SOMETHING INDECENT

SOMETHING INDECENT

Poetry Recommended by Eastern European Poets

Edited by

VALZHYNA MORT

THE POETRY FOUNDATION'S HARRIET MONROE POETRY INSTITUTE
POETS IN THE WORLD SERIES EDITOR

ILYA KAMINSKY

POETRY FOUNDATION   RED HEN PRESS | *Pasadena, CA*

Something Indecent is a publication of The Poetry Foundation and Red Hen Press. This book is published as part of the *Poets in the World* series created by The Poetry Foundation's Harriet Monroe Poetry Institute.

Book design and layout by Aly Owen and Skyler Schulze.

Library of Congress Cataloging-in-Publication Data

Something Indecent : Poetry Recommended by Eastern European Poets / edited by Valzhyna Mort, Harriet Monroe Poetry Institute.—First edition.
    pages cm.—(Poets in the World) Includes bibliographical references.
 ISBN 978-1-59709-978-3
 1. East European poetry. I. Mort, Valzhyna, 1981–
 PN849.E92S66 2013
 891.8—dc23
                                   2013024885

The Los Angeles County Arts Commission, the National Endowment for the Arts, the Pasadena Arts & Cultural Commission and the City of Pasadena Cultural Affairs Division, the Los Angeles Department of Cultural Affairs, the Dwight Stuart Youth Fund, and Sony Pictures Entertainment partially support Red Hen Press.

First Edition
Published by Red Hen Press
www.redhen.org
The Poetry Foundation
PoetryFoundation.org

In the very essence of poetry there is something indecent:
a thing is brought forth which we didn't know we had in us ...
—Czesław Miłosz, "Ars Poetica?"

Contents

FOREWORD:
STRANGE BIRDS OF EUROPE

Let me begin with the ungrateful business of speaking about the poems that speak for themselves. Seven contemporary poets from Eastern Europe (give or take a thousand miles) have shared some of their favorite European poems. Since the relationship between poetry and Europeanness is that of a bird and a cage, this is firstly an anthology of poetry selected by poets. If we cannot escape the European qualifier, let us at least agree to see this anthology as sub-European—poetry that has risen above poets' nationalities. Poetry, after all, doesn't need a passport. More so, if the temperature of the poet's imagination lowers, poetry migrates, nourishing itself on other poetic traditions. To continue with the bird metaphor, Cesare Pavese once seemed to be a *rara avis* among his Italian contemporaries—his winged muse vacationed on Walt Whitman's shoulder, overlooking his long lines, his repetitions, his subjects. Tomaž Šalamun, often described as a great postwar central European poet, has also long outgrown the borders of central Europe:

> Tomaž Šalamun is a monster.
> Tomaž Šalamun is a sphere rushing through the air.
> He lies down in twilight, he swims in twilight.
> People and I, we both look at him amazed,
> we wish him well, maybe he is a comet.

Like Pavese's muse, Šalamun's monster has made his seasonal passing through North America. In his 1998 interview with Brian Henry, Šalamun talks about his American influences: "And then the really big transformation for me was Ashbery. I read *Three Poems* and I was changed—it was something that completely fit my chemistry."

Poets selected here by no means represent European tradition—instead, they represent the tradition of reading poetry and sharing your favorite poems with friends. There was never a guarantee that somebody would pick Sappho over a hundred other choices, but Vera Pavlova did, and so the anthology opens on a proper, chronological, first-lyric-poet note (a "note" because Sappho's words sing, while I write now in mere signs).

Looking through the table of contents, I notice with great pleasure that Sappho and Catullus are not the only poets recognized by their first name. Here sit Rainer, Guillaume, César, Eugenio, Bertolt, Nâzim, Yannis, Zbigniew, Czesław, Osip,

Wisława and Marina. There are two monumental Annas, but neither of them is Akhmatova. There's Paul Celan, who should have been spared yet another anthology (but maybe not this one, okay?), and Vytautas P. Bložė, whose work is the best-kept secret from American readers.

If I entrusted this introduction solely to my imagination, I would claim that if the selected poets were themselves the selectors, we still would have ended up with a similar table of contents. Wouldn't Joseph Brodsky, the Russian John Donne, recommend John Donne? Wouldn't Marina Tsvetaeva—who sang "Rainer Maria Rilke! May I hail you like this? You, poetry incarnate, must know, after all, that your very name is a poem"—put Rilke at the top of her list? Wouldn't Anna Swir, who in "A Film About My Father" compares her artist-father to Norwid, choose Cyprian Norwid herself?

And what about others, those poets who would have made this book endless? If Rilke holds Tsvetaeva with one hand, whom does he hold with his other hand? Isn't it Ingeborg Bachmann, whose name will not appear further on these pages, but whose words bless every page to come:

> I still border on a word and on another land,
> I border, like little else, on everything more and more,
>
> a Bohemian, a wandering minstrel, who has nothing, who is held by nothing,
> gifted only at seeing, by a doubtful sea,
> the land of my choice.
> —"Bohemia Lies by the Sea," trans. by Peter Filkins

And another sea voyager, Arthur Rimbaud, sails by this book in his drunken boat, greeting and greeted by every poet here:

> Sweeter than the flesh of hard apples is to children
> The green water penetrated my hull of fir
> And washed me of spots of blue wine
> And vomit, scattering rudder and grappling-hook
>
> And from then on I bathed in the Poem
> Of the Sea, infused with stars and lactescent,

Devouring the azure verses; where, like a pale elated
Piece of flotsam, a pensive drowned figure sometimes sinks . . .
                    —"The Drunken Boat," trans. by Wallace Fowlie

But this pensive figure is not of a drowned man. It is, as E.M. Forster puts it, a "Greek gentleman in a straw hat, standing absolutely motionless at a slight angle to the universe." Constantine Cavafy—a poet Joseph Brodksy claims gains in translation—how did we lose you in this anthology? A Greek poet who, without much fuss over metaphors and rhymes, dared to rewrite Shakespeare:

[. . .] I'm walking the streets of Elsinore,
through its squares, and I recall
the very sad story
of that unfortunate king
killed by his nephew
because of some fanciful suspicions.
          —"King Claudius," trans. by Edmund Keeley and Philip Sherrard

In conclusion, I would like to point out that the introductions accompanying the poems do not mean to explain them or provide a close reading. These introductions are a gesture—a poet handing you the poem. In his essay "Le Cimetière Marin," Paul Valéry writes: "If I am questioned; if anyone wonders (as happens sometimes quite peremptorily) what I 'wanted to say' in a certain poem, I reply that I did not *want to say* but *wanted to make*, and that it was the intention of *making* which wanted what I *said.* . . ." Just the same, we didn't intend for this book to say something about European poetry. We wanted these poems to make something. What exactly? Something for all of us.

SAPPHO
Recommended by Vera Pavlova

There is only one complete extant poem by Sappho (written in the forgotten Aeolian dialect that died as far back as two thousand years ago) in addition to roughly two-hundred fragments of poems that miraculously survived destruction (most of Sappho's poems had been burned as heathen heresy). Nevertheless, Sappho enjoys the kind of fame that no poet who has ever lived on this planet has attained. She became a myth, and one of the most beloved myths at that, with painters creating her image, composers writing art songs and operas based on her destiny, and poets composing verses dedicated to her, lauding and imitating her.

In Russia, Sappho reached the peak of her fame at the beginning of the twentieth century, so much so that there was even a brand of cigarettes called "Sappho" to the delight of emancipated women. Here are some figures to testify to the incredible love for Sappho on the part of Russian authors: 150 poems have been dedicated to her (compared to seven dedicated to Ovid and two to Horace), while her "Second Ode" has enjoyed fifty-one different translations, which is the absolute record in the history of Russian poetic translations.

"He Seems to Me Equal to Gods That Man" represents a clinically accurate description of symptoms characteristic of the malady called "love," accurate to such a degree that throughout subsequent generations, people would refer to it to see if they indeed were in love, judging by presence or absence of those symptoms. Sappho's description of the symptoms cannot be called shameless, for the notion of shame is as foreign to her as to a child. That is why her lines have the purity of utterance that must have sounded in Eden, before the Fall. And we follow her contemporaries and exclaim "The divine Sappho!" although we do not have the vaguest idea of how marvelous and enchanting those lines sounded 2,600 years ago, when lyric poets still held lyres in their hands.

[HE SEEMS TO ME EQUAL TO GODS THAT MAN]

He seems to me equal to gods that man
whoever he is who opposite you
sits and listens close
    to your sweet speaking

and lovely laughing—oh it
puts the heart in my chest on wings
for when I look at you, even a moment, no speaking
    is left in me

no: tongue breaks and thin
fire is racing under skin
and in eyes no sight and drumming
    fills ears

and cold sweat holds me and shaking
grips me all, greener than grass
I am and dead—or almost
        I seem to me.

[. . .]

Translated by Anne Carson

CATULLUS
Recommended by Vera Pavlova

Half of the 116 poems consists of rough, often indecent invectives that are almost unprovoked. This is the kind of language one permits himself to speak in the circle of very close friends. I can almost see Catullus reading one of his epigrams to fellow poets who roar with laughter, and the one who laughs the loudest is the man to whom the piece pertains. What a wonderful image: a bunch of young, gifted, free, idle, and merry poets, with their capers and poetic messages, competing with and supporting each other!

The young elite of Rome had so much time for leisure that they seemed to write verses for a lack of more important things to do. Thus, it is not surprising that Catullus calls his poems "nugae," that is trifles. In the same fashion, during the nineteenth century (and already in the end of the eighteenth century), when Catullus was very much in vogue in Russia, two Russian poets, Karamzin and Dmitriev, published their collections of light verse with almost identical titles—"My Trifles" and "My Trifles, Too"—thereby insinuating that Russian poetry took lessons in writing light verse from Catullus. But did Catullus really treat his trifles all that lightly? After all, in one of his poems, he voices the wish that his poems live long: "So take this mere booklet for what it's worth, / Which may my Virgin Patroness / Keep fresh for more than one generation." Fortunately for us, that wish has come true—the sole extant copy of *The Book of Catallus of Verona* was found in the tenth century AD.

Catullus has three unlikely avatars: a bawdy poet who uses the worst of obscenities to criticize all and sundry; a scholar who diligently and at length describes obscure ancient myths; and an amorous poet who counts kisses and bemoans the death of both Lesbia's favorite sparrow and himself, betrayed by an unfaithful lover. Seen as a modernist, Catullus combines in himself all three avatars, becoming the first poet to experiment with shifting the focus from the object to the form of expression. When he curses, or engages in sophisticated discourse, or weeps, he does so with one single purpose in mind—to develop new poetic language while examining the potential for rare verse meters.

He does all that in order to find, for the first time in history, words and forms to express a man's feelings for a woman. Prior to Catullus, poets knew only how to sing the charms of their beloved, and produced their "portraits" and "sculptures." In his poems, woman is no longer a mere object of desire (in Latin, *amare* means "to love, to desire")—she becomes a companion, a tormentor, a poor soul, a bawd; she comes to life. Verses to Lesbia are a story of *Dichterliebe*, the first of its kind in history, and it is no wonder that Catullus was so much in vogue in the days of Romanticism. *Amare* alone does not suffice here, and so Catullus finds *bene velle*: benevolence, the wish not only to take, but also to give a love that gives of itself and brings into the realm of sex both the loyalty of friendship and the warmth of kinship. Catullus was the first poet frightened by love and who, for that reason, has tamed the tempestuous element of love by giving it a perfect expression.

POEM 72

There was a time, Lesbia, when
you confessed only to Catullus in love:
you would set me above Jupiter himself.
I loved you then
                not as men love their women
but as a father his children—his family.
Today I know you too well
                and desire burns deeper in me
and you are more coarse
                more frivolous in my thought.
"How," you may ask, "can this be?"
Such actions as yours excite
                increased violence of love,
Lesbia, but with friendless intention.

Translated by Peter Whigham

UNKNOWN AUTHOR
Recommended by Vera Pavlova

As readers, we are doubly fortunate to be able to enjoy the first poetic work in the history of Russian language, translated into English by a genius of both Russian and English literatures. As soon as we begin reading "The Song of Igor's Campaign," we realize that we are undoubtedly dealing with a masterpiece. It made me wonder how lines written eight hundred years ago can elicit in a reader such a vivid response today. Those lines come to life before our eyes: we see the blue lightning bolts flare, the warriors' golden helmets glitter; we hear the anxious bird-cries during the eclipse of the sun and feel the wind of the storm blow into our faces.

Nabokov, the pedant, has calculated that the eclipse foretelling Igor's defeat in the battle with the Polovets had occurred on Wednesday, May 1, 1185, at 3:25 p.m. According to his count, the text of "The Song" amounts to 14,175 letters and approximately 2,850 words. "Approximately," because in the original Russian manuscript, the words are written without spaces between them, and deciphering the text begins with breaking it into words, which leads to different versions and ambiguities, some of which still remain unresolved. But as soon as they are broken into lines (Nabokov ended up with 861, while academician Dmitry Likhachev, whose version is regarded in Russia as the most authoritative, has counted 692 lines), they turn into pure poetry not only because of the dramatic images, but also because of being so exceptionally mellifluous and vivid.

The author of "The Song" is unknown. Curiously, he not only names his poetic predecessor (and rival) Boyan by name (apparently Boyan lived in the 11th century), but also enters into a poetic polemic with him on the subject of narrative style. You might say literary rivalry was born concomitantly with the birth of literature itself. This contentious nature is what begins "The Song": the author first tells us how Boyan would have put it in his "olden" style, then parodies Boyan (who until this day is unknown to us), and then declares that he will write it in a new manner. Our ancient author appears to be an avant-garde artist!

The manuscript of "The Song" was found at the Yaroslavl Monastery of the Savior in 1790 and was bought by a private collector; later, it was burned during the Fire of Moscow in 1812. Fortunately, the collector had made a copy of it. The find was so sensational that some people suspected it to be a hoax in the style of Macpherson's *Ossian* (Nabokov and other researchers had repeatedly hinted at "the ossianism" of this masterpiece). By now, however, all suspicions on the score have been dispelled—an eminent researcher of the ancient Russian language has found in the text lexical items and grammatical structures that even the cleverest of hoaxers of later times could not possibly have known. The very suspicions of this poem serve as another proof of "The Song's" greatness—they stem from the conviction that in the semi-savage Russia, which had just become literate, such a masterpiece simply could not have been produced. "Glory to the Prince, honor to the regiment," as the poem states repeatedly. One is very much tempted to equate this unknown genius with the Prince and the glorious future poets of Russia with his regiment.

Igor had suffered a defeat, but how great was the gain of poetry for having stepped onto the field of a lost battle? From time immemorial, poetry has been better at weeping than at making merry. Igor's return and Russisches' joy over it take up only three hasty stanzas at the end of "The Song," while plenty of beautiful lines describe the misfortune that befell Rus. The best of those lines are in Euphrosyne's (the wife of Igor) lament on the ramparts of her home city, Putivl.

I have chosen this fragment, unable to include the complete text of "The Song," all 861 lines of it brilliantly translated by Nabokov. Just beware that once you begin reading it, you will not be able to put it away—no matter how wild and exotic the names and deeds of the old Russian tribes may seem to you.

EUPHROSYNE'S INCANTATION
(from "The Song of Igor's Campaign")

"I will fly, like a cuckoo," she says,
"down the Dunay.
I will dip my beaver sleeve
in the river Kayala.
I will wipe the bleeding wounds
on the prince's hardy body."
Yaroslav's daughter early weeps,
in Putivl on the rampart, repeating:

"Wind, Great Wind!
Why, lord, blow perversely?
Why carry those Hinish dartlets
on your light winglets
against my husband's warriors?
Are you not satisfied
to blow on high, up to the clouds,
rocking the ships upon the blue sea?
Why, lord, have you dispersed
my gladness all over the feather grass?"
Yaroslav's daughter early weeps,
in Putivl on the rampart, repeating:

"O Dnepr, famed one!
You have pierced stone hills
through the Kuman land.
You have lolled upon you
Svyatoslav's galleys
as far as Kobyaka's camp.
Loll up to me, lord, my husband
that I may not send my tears
seaward thus early."
Yaroslav's daughter early weeps,
in Putivl on the rampart, repeating:

"Bright and thrice-bright Sun!
To all you are warm and comely;
Why spread, lord, your scorching rays
on [my] husband's warriors;
[why] in the waterless field
parch their bows
with thirst,
close their quivers
with anguish?"

Translated by Vladimir Nabokov

KING DAVID
Recommended by Vera Pavlova

What was the very first poem in the world? My answer is the Psalter, with its praises for God and admiration for His creation, complaints and supplication, triumph of victors, and lamentation of the vanquished. All of that was an integral part of singing, of playing musical instruments, and of dancing. I get dizzy when I imagine David dancing (or simply jumping from unbearable joy!), half-naked in front of the reliquary containing the Testament! At that moment, he was not just the Poet, he was poetry incarnate.

For Russian poetry, the Psalter has been of crucial importance. It was translated into Russian in the eleventh century by Cyril and Methodius, the two Greek monks who had invented the Cyrillic alphabet. The Psalter and the Primer were the two books that had helped Old Russia learn how to read. Then, in the seventeenth century, Simeon Polotsky's Psalter came to Russia from the Grand Duchy of Lithuania; Russian poets started using it to learn the accentual-syllabic versification. It took the efforts of several generations of authors to establish the practice of the verse-meter system that today seems as unshakable as a law of nature. And here again King David was instrumental: in 1752, a controversy among the Russian writers flared up as to what verse meter was more appropriate for poetry of the lofty style, the iamb or the trochee. To settle the matter, the three leading poets of the day (Lomonosov, Sumarokov, and Trediakovsky) took "Psalm 144," and each of them rendered it in accentual-syllabic verses of different meters. All three versions were published without indicating their authors, and the reading public was to decide which version was the best. Lomonosov, the most talented of the three poets, was pronounced the winner, and thus the iamb became the unofficial state meter in Russia.

King David will forever be the foremost poet of Europe. Even in translations, the poetic merits of his Psalms are obvious—the beauty and grandeur of imagery, the fierce energy of repetitions and intensifications, the lofty pathos and simplicity, the liberal combining of the earthly with the heavenly, of the abstract with the quotidian.

PSALM 144
(King James Version)

Blessed be the LORD my strength, which teacheth my hands to war, and
    my fingers to fight:

My goodness, and my fortress; my high tower, and my deliverer; my shield,
    and he in whom I trust; who subdueth my people under me.

LORD, what is man, that thou takest knowledge of him! or the son of man,
    that thou makest account of him!

Man is like to vanity: his days are as a shadow that passeth away.

Bow thy heavens, O LORD, and come down: touch the mountains, and
    they shall smoke.

Cast forth lightning, and scatter them: shoot out thine arrows, and
    destroy them.

Send thine hand from above; rid me, and deliver me out of great waters,
    from the hand of strange children;

Whose mouth speaketh vanity, and their right hand is a right hand
    of falsehood.

I will sing a new song unto thee, O God: upon a psaltery and an instrument
    of ten strings will I sing praises unto thee.

It is he that giveth salvation unto kings: who delivereth David his servant
    from the hurtful sword.

Rid me, and deliver me from the hand of strange children, whose mouth
    speaketh vanity, and their right hand is a right hand of falsehood:

That our sons may be as plants grown up in their youth; that our daughters
    may be as corner stones, polished after the similitude of a palace:

That our garners may be full, affording all manner of store: that our sheep
    may bring forth thousands and ten thousands in our streets:

That our oxen may be strong to labor; that there be no breaking in, nor
    going out; that there be no complaining in our streets.

Happy is that people, that is in such a case: yea, happy is that people, whose
    God is the LORD.

JOHN DONNE

Recommended by Vera Pavlova

Russian readers have learned of John Donne's name from the epigraph to Hemingway's *For Whom the Bell Tolls*. The name was easy to remember, being consonant with the Russian imitation of the tolling bell's sound: "don-don." At the time, there were no translations of Donne's work; they appeared only around the middle of the twentieth century. Joseph Brodsky was one of the first to begin translating Donne. The future Nobel Prize winner was a little over twenty years old when he signed a contract for translating English metaphysical poets. He did not complete the project because of his expulsion from the USSR. As for his juvenile translations, they are far from accurate, and in them Brodsky was just beginning to get the feel of Donne's intonation. In the West, Brodsky did not continue working on those translations, although Donne has forever remained a beacon for him. Having failed at becoming the translator of Donne, Brodsky instead became "the Russian John Donne," the most eminent representative of metaphysical poetry in Russian literature. The Russian translators of Donne who came after Brodsky have acquired the tonality of Brodksy's Russian poems; as a result, their translations of Donne often sound like poems by Brodsky.

This is not surprising—they had no other paradigms on which to fall in the Russian tradition (except, perhaps, Derzhavin, a Russian baroque poet of the eighteenth century). Russian poetry had opted for the way of "beautiful clarity" and melodiousness. It was not prone to cultivate wit, the cornerstone of the metaphysical school, defined by Baltasar Gracián in *The Art of Worldly Wisdom* (1642) as follows: "the mastery of wit consists in elegant and harmonious combining and juxtaposing two or three remote notions that are connected through a single effort of the mind." Wit of that sort can overcome the sense of loss of the world's wholeness. Donne formulates that loss in "An Anatomy of the World": "'Tis all in pieces, all coherence gone." He speaks of the crumbling world, of the vanishing sun, regretting that it is not given to the human mind to restore the wholeness ("and no man's wit / Can well direct him, where to look for it").

At the same time, neither man nor poet has anything to which he can pin his hopes, other than an astute wit that seeks and finds the needed connections, even if they are quite remote. Wit is an ability, while *concetti* (i.e. metaphors that closely bring together seemingly unrelated objects and notions) are the tools of thought accessible to no one but a poet. Donne's (and Brodsky's) poetics can thus be concisely described as the concentration of meaning (metaphorism), a dramatic and profoundly personal situation of a lyrical monologue (conversational tone), and the construction of text as a sequence of witty arguments (in which *concetti* serve as proofs). These poetics are supplemented with meditation as defined by Ignatius of Loyola: "we can converse with God the way a servant converses with his Master, a son with his Father, a friend with his friend, a wife with her beloved husband, a criminal with his Judge, or in some other way, as the Holy Spirit may instruct us."

"A Valediction: Forbidding Mourning" is one of the few of Donne's poems that Brodsky finished translating. As required by tradition, the poem is addressed to the poet's wife, prior to Donne's departure for France in 1611. Just as many other of Donne's poems, it is written in the form of a logical argument in support of the idea that two people who love each other cannot possibly be separated. The steps in the argument are a chain of metaphors that bring together the eternal and the everyday. Just as a theorem in geometry, the consoling thought is reinforced with the help of a compass. Igor Shaitanov, an influencial Russian literary critic, theorist, and editor writes: "The baroque rationalism directs the mind and the rhetoric toward exploring the irrational; it builds a harmonious construction over the abyss of being that gravitates toward chaos."

A VALEDICTION: FORBIDDING MOURNING

As virtuous men pass mildly away,
    And whisper to their souls to go,
Whilst some of their sad friends do say,
    "The breath goes now" and some say, "No";

So let us melt, and make no noise,
    No tear-floods, nor sigh-tempests move,
'Twere profanation of our joys
    To tell the laity our love.

Moving of th' earth brings harms and fears,
    Men reckon what it did, and meant,
But trepidation of the spheres,
    Though greater far, is innocent.

Dull sublunary lovers' love
    (Whose soul is sense) cannot admit
Absence, 'cause it doth remove
    Those things which elemented it.

But we by a love, so much refined,
    That our selves know not what it is,
Inter-assured of the mind,
    Care less, eyes, lips, and hands to miss.

Our two souls therefore, which are one,
    Though I must go, endure not yet
A breach, but an expansion,
    Like gold to airy thinness beat.

If they be two, they are two so
    As stiff twin compasses are two,
Thy soul, the fixed foot, makes no show
    To move, but doth, if th' other do.

And though it in the centre sit,
    Yet when the other far doth roam,
It leans, and hearkens after it,
    And grows erect, as that comes home.

Such wilt thou be to me, who must
    Like th' other foot, obliquely run;
Thy firmness makes my circle just,
    And makes me end, where I begun.

Cyprian Norwid
Recommended by Vera Pavlova

Cyprian Kamil Norwid was born in the fall of 1821 and orphaned in early childhood (he lost his mother at the age of four, his father at the age of fourteen, and his native country at the age of twenty). His life after that, replete with adversities, was that of a wandering emigrant, a citizen of the world, without any rights of citizenship. Norwid lived in Dresden, Paris, Brussels, London, Venice, and even New York. It is hard to find another poet more European in the literal geographic sense of the word, with his native Poland being the only country off limits to him—the Russian government stripped Norwid of his citizenship and confiscated his property. Longing for homeland was as familiar to him as it was to Chopin, whom he had met in Paris and on whose death he wrote a splendid poem entitled "Chopin's Piano." Norwid died in 1883 in the suburbs of Paris, at St. Casimir, a hospice for poor and elderly Polish exiles, in total oblivion, deaf and blind. Most of his poems remained in manuscripts until they were published as late as the 1920s and 1930s. Some of his poetic output has been irrevocably lost.

The discovery of Norwid as a poet was a sensation. After the Second World War, all Polish poetry grew under the impact of Norwid's legacy, which can be seen not only in the poetry of the Nobel Prize winners Miłosz and Szymborska, but also that of many other Polish poets, as different from each other as Grochowiak, Herbert, Różewicz, or Zagajewski. All of them have inherited what brings Norwid close to Lermontov and what the latter called "verses drenched with bitterness and wrath," of which Norwid had plenty. In one of his last poems, however, written at the hospice and on the subject of that hospice, Norwid writes: "Everything on this earth passes, only poetry and kindness remain, nothing else."

In his essay published in a magazine *Inostrannaya Literatura*, 6, 2002, Anatoliy Geleskul, a Russian translator of Norwid, writes:

> Norwid's ascetic poetry thrives on thought, at times it is oversaturated with thought, but almost always thought is at that poetry's inception; left in its incomplete state, thought seems to be searching for itself in the thickets of doubts and impasses. Some of his poems simply bristle with antinomies as with needles, and they are hard to handle. We find an expressive simile on this score in one of

Norwid's poems: thought is like a painter's canvas that has not yet dried out, and though finished, it should not be touched before its time comes.

Out of the numerous wonderful poems by Norwid, I have selected "Marionettes," which he wrote onboard the seafaring ship *Marguerita*, sailing to New York from London, on December 1852 at 10 a.m. (as the author indicates in the manuscript).

MARIONETTES

I

How can one not feel bored when millions
Of silent stars are glowing above the planet,
Each of them different, when all creation
Is at a standstill and yet soaring . . .

II

The earth is also still, so is the void of ages,
And all those who are alive at the moment,
Of whom not the minutest bone will endure,
Though people will still exist, as always . . .

III

One cannot but feel bored on the stage so little
And so imperfectly built, where all and sundry
Ideals have been staged, and where
Your life is the price of the performance—

IV

Verily, I know not how to bide my time here,
Accosted as I am by sheer boredom.
How should I cope with it, dear Lady?
Am I to write prose, or maybe verses?

V

Or should I forego writing altogether . . .
Just sit in bright sunshine, read the curious novel
That the Deluge has written on the sand's granules
For people's amusement, I reckon (!)—

VI

Or, better yet, for that accursed boredom,
I know a remedy still more effective:
To forget people, to call on notables,
—To sport a cravat, smartly knotted . . . !

Translated by Steven Seymour

PAUL VALÉRY
Recommended by Adam Zagajewski

This is a very famous poem. I must confess: it's the only poem by Paul Valéry that I cherish. It's a great poem, a great meditation on time and life, on the beauty of the world and the destruction thereof. There's a new translation of this poem by Derek Mahon, maybe not the most faithful one, but strong, muscular, vivid. We read it in our seminar a couple of years ago in Chicago (Fall 2011), and it took us plenty of time to decipher the complex meaning of the poem, but when we finally arrived at the brilliant and invigorating closure and I asked the class "was it worth it?" there was no sign of hesitation in their answer.

THE SEASIDE CEMETERY
Derek Mahon
(A version of "Le Cimetière marin" by Paul Valéry)

> *Do not aspire to immortal life, my soul,*
> *but exhaust the field of the possible.*
> —Pindar

I

A tranquil surface where a spinnaker moves
flickers among the pines, among the graves;
objective noon films with its fiery gaze
a shifting sea, drifters like pecking doves,
and my reward for thought is a long gaze
down the blue silence of celestial groves.

II

When, as now, light freezes above the gulf,
a gem revolving in its radiant gleam
such many-faceted and glittering foam
that a great peace seems to extend itself,
those clear-cut artifacts of the continuum,
time and knowledge, take the shape of a dream.

III

Wide-open vault and chaste shrine to Athene,
deep reservoir of calmly shining money,
like an eye the supercilious water-structure
lies somnolent beneath its burning veils;
and my soul-silence too is architecture,
a golden hoard roofed with a thousand tiles.

IV

Temple of time I breathe when I breathe in,
to this high point I climb and feel at home
ordering all things with a seaward stare
of circumspection; and, as my supreme
offering to the gods, the serene glare
sows on the depths an imperious disdain.

V

But even as fruit consumes itself in taste,
even as it translates its own demise
deliciously in the mouth where its form dies,
I sniff already my own future smoke
while light sings to the ashen soul the quick
change starting now on the murmuring coast.

VI

Under this clear sky it is I who change—
after so much conceit, after such strange
lassitude, but bursting with new power,
I give myself up to these brilliant spaces;
on the mansions of the dead my shadow oases
reminding me of its own ephemeral hour.

VII

A soul-exposure to the solar torches
I can endure, and the condign tortures
of the midsummer's pitiless bronze light;
and though submission show a midnight face
invisible in daytime, to that bright
presence I concede the superior place.

VIII

Stopped at a cistern with a pumping heart
between the vacuum and the creative act
whispering to my preliminary tact,
I await the echo of an interior force,
that bitter, dark and sonorous water-source
ringing in depth beyond the reach of art.

IX

Caged though you seem behind a mesh of branches,
great gulf, consumer of these meagre fences,
a blinding secret on the lids, reveal
what body draws me to its indolences,
what face invites me to this bony soil.
A faint spark ponders these inheritances.

X

Composed of sombre trees, of light and stone,
an earthly splinter held up to the sun,
sacred, enclosed in immaterial fire,
I like this place with its dark poplar flames,
the marble glimmering in the shadows here
where a faithful sea snores on the table-tombs.

XI

And if, sole shepherd, with a pastoral eye
I gaze too long on these mysterious flocks,
on these white souls, each in its tranquil box,
may the sea's growl dispel the idolatrous things,
frightening off the prudent doves, the coy
illusions and the angels' curious wings.

XII

The future, here already, scarcely moves.
A quick insect scratches the dry leaves;
everything is exhausted, scorched by the air
into I don't know what rigorous form.
Dazed with diversity, the enormous swarm
of life is bittersweet and the mind clear.

XIII

The hidden dead lie easy in this soil
which holds them tight and seasons their mystique;
high up the southern noon, completely still,
reflects upon itself where none may look.
Absolute monarch, firmament of blue,
I am the secret difference now in you.

XIV

I am the one your worst fears validate—
my cowardice, my bad thoughts, my contrition
make up the one flaw in your precious opal;
and meanwhile, in a dense marmoreal night
among the roots, a vague oceanic people
have long ago arrived at your conclusion.

XV

Mixed in a thick solution underground
the white clay is drunk by crimson kind;
its vigor circulates in the veined flowers.
Where now are the colloquial turns of phrase,
the individual gifts and singular souls?
Where once a tear gathered the grub crawls.

XVI

The ticklish virgins with their twittering cries,
the teeth, the eyelids and the gentle eyes,
enchanted breasts heaving in provocation,
glistening lips shiny with invitation,
the last delights, the fingers that resist,
all join the circle and return to dust.

XVII

And you, great soul, dare you hypostasize
a world untarnished by the luminous lies
the sun and sea suggest to mortal eyes?
Will you still sing when you've become a ghost?
Nonsense, everything flows, ourselves the most;
the hunger for eternity also dies.

XVIII

Gaunt immortality, gold inscribed on black,
cold consolation crowned with a laurel wreath
that makes a maternal bosom of grim death,
a gorgeous fiction and a lugubrious joke—
who doesn't know, and who would not decline
the empty skull with its eternal grin?

XIX

Archaic progenitors, your derelict heads
returned to pasture by so many spades,
no longer knowing the familiar tread—
the real ravager, the irrefutable worm
is not for you, at rest now in the tomb;
it lives on life and never leaves my side.

XX

Self-love, self-hatred, what's the difference?
Its secret mordancy is so intense
the silent gnawing goes by many names.
Watching, desiring, nibbling, considering,
it likes the flesh and, even in my dreams,
I live on sufferance of this ravenous thing.

XXI

Zeno, harsh theorist of conceptual zero,
have you transfixed me with your winged arrow
which quivers, flies, yet doesn't fly at all?
Does the twang wake me and the arrow kill?
Sunlight, is it merely a tortoise-shade,
the mighty hero frozen in mid-stride?

XXII

No, no; get up; go on to the next phase—
body, shake off this meditative pose
and, chest, inhale the first flap of the air.
A palpable new freshness off the sea,
an ozone rush, restores my soul to me
and draws me down to the reviving shore.

XXIII

Great sea endowed with frenzy and sensation,
slick panther-hide and heaving vegetation
sown with a million images of the sun;
unchained monster drunk on your blue skin,
chewing for ever your own glistening tail
in a perpetual, silent-seeming turmoil—

XXIV

the wind rises; it's time to start. A stiff breeze
opens and shuts the notebook on my knees
and powdery waves explode among the rocks
flashing; fly off, then, my sun-dazzled pages
and break, waves, break up with ecstatic surges
this shifting surface where the spinnaker flocks!

RAINER MARIE RILKE
Recommended by Vera Pavlova

Rilke. If you pronounce the name many times in a row, it will sound like "Lyriker" ("lyrical poet" in German). Rilke is a poet par excellence, the most complete embodiment of the myth of a poet, as it has formed over the many thousands of years that poetry has existed. "The best poet of Europe" (Emile Verhaeren); "the very essence of poetry" (Marina Tsvetaeva). When I started thinking about my future recommendations, Rilke's name was the first that I put down in my notebook.

That list is nearing its end, and just as in the final scene of Mozart's operas, all characters appear on the stage, every single string of the European lyre sings in Rilke's poetry. David, the psalm singer? Here he is, in the poem "David Sings to Saul." Sappho? Here is her voice, in "Sappho an Alkaios." St. Ephraim, the Syrian? He is in *The Book of Hours*, every poem of which is a pure prayer, and an effective prayer at that. "The Song of Igor's Campaign"? Rilke did a complete translation of it. Petrarch? Rilke has translated two of his sonnets. Louise Labe? He translated all of the twenty-four sonnets she had written. Norwid? Rilke was one of the first to give high praise to the Pole's talent.

And Russia? For Rilke, Russia was a promised land. Of Russia, he said that while all countries bordered other countries, Russia bordered God. He visited Russia, had meetings with Tolstoy, and learned Russian. He even wrote poems in Russian, in rhymed verse! All Russian poetry snobs (including myself) know those poems by heart; their funny grammatical blunders not withstanding, those verses glow with poetry.

I fell in love with Rilke from the first line of his that I read. In a little poem I wrote when I was twenty-five, I confessed that I loved Rilke because "I do not speak German, / but translators, it seems, distort him." Indeed, in Rilke's poems, poetry glows through any translation, no matter how inaccurate or clumsy that translation may be. Arguably, no poet has been translated as often as Rilke—I have come across an essay entitled "The Panther: A comparison of one hundred translations in fifteen languages." His poem entitled "The Panther" came out in Russia as a separate book containing the original, a literal translation, and dozens of various translated versions. Such is the great desire to solve the mystery of Rilke's poetry, or at least to get closer to that mystery. One has the impression that if we comprehended that mystery, we would also understand something even more significant, essential, something that is at the very core of our existence—although, perhaps, there is nothing more significant or essential than the mystery of poetry.

The poem "Orpheus. Eurydice. Hermes" I found in two dozen translations. I have read six of them, and six times I got a lump in my throat and tears in my eyes whenever I got to the line "she could not understand, and softly answered / Who?"

Brodsky pronounced this poem the best written in the twentieth century and dedicated to it an extensive essay entitled "Ninety Years Later." I will refrain from analyzing this poem; all I want to do is read and reread it endlessly, from beginning to end, while reading it to learn, with the humility of Eurydice, the sacred craft, the skill of creating worlds out of the amorphous realm of words. In the manner of Orpheus. The way Rilke did.

ORPHEUS. EURYDICE. HERMES

That was the deep uncanny mine of souls.
Like veins of silver ore, they silently
moved through its massive darkness. Blood welled up
among the roots, on its way to the world of men,
and in the dark it looked as hard as stone.
Nothing else was red.

There were cliffs there,
and forests made of mist. There were bridges
spanning the void, and that great gray blind lake
which hung above its distant bottom
like the sky on a rainy day above a landscape.
And through the gentle, unresisting meadows
one pale path unrolled like a strip of cotton.

Down this path they were coming.

In front, the slender man in the blue cloak—
mute, impatient, looking straight ahead.
In large, greedy, unchewed bites his walk
devoured the path; his hands hung at his sides,

tight and heavy, out of the failing folds,
no longer conscious of the delicate lyre
which had grown into his left arm, like a slip
of roses grafted onto an olive tree.
His senses felt as though they were split in two:
his sight would race ahead of him like a dog,
stop, come back, then rushing off again
would stand, impatient, at the path's next turn,—
but his hearing, like an odor, stayed behind.
Sometimes it seemed to him as though it reached
back to the footsteps of those other two
who were to follow him, up the long path home.
But then, once more, it was just his own steps' echo,
or the wind inside his cloak, that made the sound.
He said to himself, they had to be behind him;
said it aloud and heard it fade away.
They had to be behind him, but their steps
were ominously soft. If only he could
turn around, just once (but looking back
would ruin this entire work, so near
completion), then he could not fail to see them,
those other two, who followed him so softly:

The god of speed and distant messages,
a traveler's hood above his shining eyes,
his slender staff held out in front of him,
and little wings fluttering at his ankles;
and on his left arm, barely touching it: *she.*

A woman so loved that from one lyre there came
more lament than from all lamenting women;
that a whole world of lament arose, in which
all nature reappeared: forest and valley,

road and village, field and stream and animal;
and that around this lament-world, even as
around the other earth, a sun revolved
and a silent star-filled heaven, a lament-
heaven, with its own, disfigured stars—:
So greatly was she loved.

But now she walked beside the graceful god,
her steps constricted by the trailing graveclothes,
uncertain, gentle, and without impatience.
She was deep within herself, like a woman heavy
with child, and did not see the man in front
or the path ascending steeply into life.
Deep within herself. Being dead
filled her beyond fulfillment. Like a fruit
suffused with its own mystery and sweetness,
she was filled with her vast death, which was so new,
she could not understand that it had happened.

She had come into a new virginity
and was untouchable; her sex had closed
like a young flower at nightfall, and her hands
had grown so unused to marriage that the god's
infinitely gentle touch of guidance
hurt her, like an undesired kiss.

She was no longer that woman with blue eyes
who once had echoed through the poet's songs,
no longer the wide couch's scent and island,
and that man's property no longer.

She was already loosened like long hair,
poured out like fallen rain,
shared like a limitless supply.

She was already root.

And when, abruptly,
the god put out his hand to stop her, saying,
with sorrow in his voice: He has turned around—,
she could not understand, and softly answered
Who?

       Far away,
dark before the shining exit-gates,
someone or other stood, whose features were
unrecognizable. He stood and saw
how, on the strip of road among the meadows,
with a mournful look, the god of messages
silently turned to follow the small figure
already walking back along the path,
her steps constricted by the trailing graveclothes,
uncertain, gentle, and without impatience.

Translated by Stephen Mitchell

ANTONIO MACHADO
Recommended by Adam Zagajewski

The last lines of this self-portrait have—for me—a magical force: like *hijos de la mar,* "children of the sea," boys no more than fifteen years old, who I saw jumping in and out of the not very pristine waters of the Bosporus in Istanbul. Machado is someone the Spaniards love more than any other poet. Many ingredients of his poetry do well in translation (though unrhymed translations are perhaps better than the more formal ones). In this particular poem, the final gesture is absolutely splendid: first we get a rich and slightly ironic texture of the poet's life, and later all this vanishes not in any kind of theatrical "look how I die" aria, but in a discreet disappearance, as if this meaningful life had simply vanished in the ocean.

PORTRAIT

My childhood is memories of a patio in Sevilla
and a shining orchard where the lemon tree ripens.
My youth, twenty years on the earth of Castilla,
my life, a few events that I prefer forgotten.

Not a seducing Don Juan or a Bradomín—
by now you know the shabby plainness of my dress—
but I was hit by Cupid's arrow and have been
in love whenever women fed me welcomeness.

Coursing my veins are drops of Jacobinic blood,
and yet my poems issue from a tranquil fountain;
more than an upright man who knows his doctrine,
I am, in the good meaning of the word, good.

I love beauty and in tune with modern aesthetics,
have plucked old roses from the garden of Ronsard,
but I don't love the rouge of contrived cosmetics,
and am no chirping bird in the latest garb.

I scorn the ballads of loud tenors as hollow
as a choir of crickets singing to the moon.
I stop to note the voices from their echo
and among those voices listen to only one.

Am I romantic or classical? I don't know.
I'd like to leave my verse as a captain his blade,
known for the iron hand that made it glow,
not for the maker's celebrated mark or trade.

I chat with a companion with me to the end—
who speaks alone may hope to speak to God one day,
and my soliloquy is chat with that good friend
who showed me secrets of a philanthropic way.

And in the end I owe you nothing. For what I write
you owe *me*. I go to work, pay for the house I rent,
the suit that covers me, the cot I lie on at night,
and the plain bread that gives me nourishment.

And when the day for my final voyage arrives,
and the ship, never to return, is set to leave,
you will find me on board, light on supplies,
and almost naked like the children of the sea.

Translated by Willis Barnstone

GUILLAUME APOLLINAIRE
Recommended by Adam Zagajewski

Guillaume Apollinaire was a French poet who for a long time had no homeland. His Polish mother, an adventuress, as she's usually called (the father was absent), sent him to a French school, where the French language eventually become his *patria*. It's widely known that he stood in the center of the Parisian and European avant-garde movements; a friend of Picasso, he supported and even invented new "isms." But, less well known, faith in the meaning and spiritual success of these movements was not very strong in the inner chambers of the poet's heart. In two of his greatest poems, "Zone" and "The Pretty Redhead," joy of a new discovery, of the newness of modernity, is mixed with many questions, even with despair. I find it fascinating, this combination of faith in the youthfulness and basic rightness of the avant-garde movement and doubt, with black forebodings, as if Apollinaire, who had a short life (he died at age forty on the day WWI ended—and when Parisian crowds yelled "Down with Guillaume,"—the French version of the German Kaiser's name, Wilhelm) knew something about the future, about the terror this century was about to produce, something that his comrades (poets and painters flourishing at the beginning of the century) didn't have a hint of.

THE PRETTY REDHEAD
James Wright
from the French of Apollinaire

I stand here in the sight of everyone a man full of sense
Knowing life and knowing of death what a living man can know
Having gone through the griefs and happinesses of love
Having known sometimes how to impose his ideas
Knowing several languages
Having traveled more than a little
Having seen war in the artillery and the infantry
Wounded in the head trepanned under chloroform
Having lost his best friends in the horror of battle

I know as much as one man alone can know
Of the ancient and the new
And without troubling myself about this war today
Between us and for us my friends
I judge this long quarrel between tradition and imagination
Between order and adventure

You whose mouth is made in the image of God's mouth
Mouth which is order itself
Judge kindly when you compare us
With those who were the very perfection of order
We who are seeking everywhere for adventure

We are not your enemies
Who want to give ourselves vast strange domains
Where mystery flowers into any hands that long for it
Where there are new fires colors never seen
A thousand fantasies difficult to make sense out of
They must be made real
All we want is to explore kindness the enormous country where
        everything is silent
And there is time which somebody can banish or welcome home
Pity for us who fight always on the frontiers
Of the illimitable and the future
Pity our mistakes pity our sins

Here summer is coming the violent season
And so my youth is as dead as spring
Oh Sun it is the time of reason grown passionate
And I am still waiting
To follow the forms she takes noble and gentle
So I may love her alone

She comes and draws me as a magnet draws filaments of iron
She has the lovely appearance
Of an adorable redhead
Her hair turns golden you would say
A beautiful lightning flash that goes on and on
Or the flames that spread out their feathers
In wilting tea roses

But laugh laugh at me
Men everywhere especially people from here
For there are so many things that I don't dare to tell you
So many things that you would not let me say
Have pity on me

GOTTFRIED BENN
Recommended by Adam Zagajewski

It's hard to choose the best Gottfried Benn poem. He said in an essay that a great poet is someone who writes perhaps five or six great poems in his or her lifetime. He wrote more than that, though not many among his poems survived the pain of travel to English. I like Chopin so much, and this Benn poem is for me a masterly representation of his music. Music cannot be represented in print, cannot be paraphrased, even suggested. Yet when Benn writes about Chopin's life, his poem is a kind of very short biography of the composer, and through the chinks in the poem's structure, we learn something about Chopin's music. A delicate knowledge is instilled through this poem.

CHOPIN

Not much of a conversationalist,
ideas weren't his strong suit,
ideas miss the point,
when Delacroix expounded his theories
it made him nervous, he for his part
could offer no explanation of the Nocturnes.

A poor lover;
mere shadow in Nohant
where George Sand's children
rejected his attempts
at discipline.

His tuberculosis
took the chronic form,
with repeated bleeding and scarring;
a creeping death,
as opposed to one
in convulsions of agony
or by firing squad:

the piano (Erard) was pushed back against the door
and Delphine Potocka
sang him
a violet song in his last hour.

He took three pianos with him to England:
Pleyel, Erard, Broadwood,
for twenty guineas
he would give fifteen-minute recitals in the evenings
at the Rothschilds' and the Wellingtons', in Strafford House
to the assembled cummerbunds;
then, dark with fatigue and imminent death,
he went home
to the Square d'Orleans.

Then he burned his sketches
and manuscripts,
didn't want any leftover scraps
betraying him—
at the end he said:
"I have taken my experiment
as far as it was possible for me to go."

Each finger was to play
to no more than its natural strength,
the fourth being the weakest
(twinned with the middle finger).
At the start, they occupied the keys
of E, F sharp, G sharp, B and C.

Anyone hearing
certain of his Preludes
in country seats or

at altitude,
through open French windows
on the terrace, say, of a sanatorium,
will not easily forget it.

He composed no operas,
no symphonies,
only those tragic progressions
from artistic conviction
and with a small hand.

Translated by Michael Hofmann

SAINT-JOHN PERSE
Recommended by Valzhyna Mort

Alexis Léger wrote *Anabasis* during his diplomatic years in China. Later the poem was pulled out randomly by his friend from a stack of manuscripts and published, thus saved from oblivion; the rest of the manuscript was later confiscated by the Nazis. It was the first poem Léger signed as Saint-John Perse, a poet who became a great influence on T.S. Eliot and R.M. Rilke. *Anabasis* will baffle you with its ceremonial, old-fashioned language that paradoxically manages to contain in itself Perse's unstoppable, untamable imagination. Canto V (the poem consists of ten cantos) is a nocturne, a song for the solitude of a man of action, a nomad, builder of a new city, leader of migration.

V (from "Anabasis")

For my soul engaged in far matters, in towns an hundred fires revived by the
    barking of dogs . . .
Solitude! our immoderate partisans boasted of our ways, but our thoughts
    were already encamped beneath other walls:
"I have told no one to wait . . . I hate you all, gently. . . . And what is to be said
    of this song that you elicit from us? . ."
Leader of a people of dreams to be led to the Dead Seas, where shall I find
    the water of night that shall bathe our eyes?
Solitude! . . squadrons of stars pass the edge of the world, enlisting from the
    kitchens a homely star.
The Confederate Kings of Heaven make war over my roof and, lords of the
    high places, set there their bivouacs.
Let me go alone with the airs of the night, among the pamphleteering
    Princes, among the falling Bielides! . .
Soul united in silence to the bitumen of the Dead! our eyelids sewn with
    needles! praised be the waiting under our eyelids!
The night gives its milk, O take heed! let a honeyed finger touch the lips of
    the prodigal:
". . . Fruit of woman, O Sabaean! . ." Betraying the least sober soul and
    roused from the pure pestilences of night,

in my thoughts I will protest against the activity of dream; I shall be off
    with the wild geese, in the sick smell of morning! . .
Ah when the star was benighted in the servant-girls' quarters, did we know
    that already so many new spears
pursued in the desert the silicates of Summer? "Dawn, you were saying . . ."
    Ablutions on the banks of the Dead Seas!
Those who lay naked in the enormous season arise in crowd on the earth—
    arise in crowds and cry out
that this world is mad! . . The old man stirs his eyelids in the yellow light;
    the woman extends herself from nail to nail;
and the gummed colt thrusts his bearded chin into the hand of the child, to
    whom it does not yet occur to knock out one of his eyes . . .
"Solitude! I have told no one to wait . . . I shall go away in that direction when
    I wish . . ."—And the Stranger clothed
in his new thoughts, acquires still more partisans in the ways of silence: his
    eye is full of a sort of spittle,
there is no more substance of man in him. And the earth in its winged seeds,
    like a poet in his thoughts, travels . . .

Translated by T.S. Eliot

GEORG TRAKL
Recommended by Nikola Madzirov

"Silence in the rented room," wrote Trakl, and again he framed an image inside his fear of pain. I would rather be a pilgrim in the empty space among Trakl's verbal sketches and colors; I would rather have the sun fall asleep each dawn upon the moss of the roof of the house where I return—a future museum of broken suitcases and steps.

THE SUN

Each day the gold sun comes over the hill.
The woods are beautiful, also the dark animals,
Also man; hunter or farmer.
The fish rises with a red body in the green pond.
Under the arch of heaven
The fisherman travels smoothly in his blue skiff.
The grain, the cluster of grapes, ripens slowly.
When the still day comes to an end,
Both evil and good have been prepared.
When the night has come,
Easily the pilgrim lifts his heavy eyelids;
The sun breaks from gloomy ravines.

DESCENT AND DEFEAT

To Karl Borromaus Heinrich

Over the white fishpond
The wild birds have blown away.
An icy wind drifts from our stars at evening.
Over our graves
The broken forehead of the night is bending.
Under the oaks we veer in a silver skiff.
The white walls of the city are always giving off sound.
Under arching thorns
O my brother blind minute-hands we are climbing
toward midnight.

Translated by Robert Bly and James Wright

János Pilinszky
Recommended by Adam Zagajewski

I know this poem in the English translation by Ted Hughes. Pilinszky was a Hungarian poet, a Catholic, if I remember correctly, who during WWII saw some of the atrocities for which this war was famous (or infamous). Unlike Radnóti, who perished toward the end of the war—and whose final poems were found in his coat pocket months after the poet's demise—Pilinszky was given the chance to live a longer life, to write down in peace (in the relative peace of a Communist country) his remembrances from the time of horror. This is a poem of observation, an observation filled with pity and empathy. It shows a rare capacity for opening up to a neighbor. We only know that the person in question was a "French prisoner," and that he was very hungry. But it's basically a poem that builds a bridge between strangers, a poem that undoes the terrifying anonymity of collective suffering—which, this very undoing, is obviously poetry's ambitious task.

The French Prisoner

If only I could forget him, the Frenchman
I saw outside our quarters, creeping round
near daybreak in that density of garden
as if he'd almost grown into the ground.
He was just looking back, peering about him
to check that he was safe here and alone:
once he was sure, his plunder was all his!
Whatever chanced, he'd not be moving on.

He was already eating. He was wolfing
a pilfered turnip hidden in his rags.
Eating raw cattle feed. But he'd no sooner
swallowed a mouthful than it made him gag;
and the sweet food encountered on his tongue
delight and then disgust, as it might be
the unhappy and the happy, meeting in
their bodies' all-consuming ecstasy.

Only forget that body . . . Shoulder blades
trembling, and a hand all skin and bone,
the palm cramming his mouth in such a way
that it too seemed to feed in clinging on.
And then the furious and desperate shame
of organs galled with one another, forced
to tear from one another what should bind them
together in community at last.

The way his clumsy feet had been left out
of all that gibbering bestial joy; and how
they stood splayed out and paralyzed beneath
the body's torture and fierce rapture now.
And his look too—if I could forget that!
Retching, he went on gobbling as if driven
on and on, just to eat, no matter what,
anything, this or that, himself even.
Why go on? It turned out that he'd escaped
from the prison camp nearby—guards came for him.
I wander, as I did then in that garden,
among my garden shadows here at home.
"If only I could forget him, the Frenchman"—
I'm looking through my notes, I read one out,
and from my ears, my eyes, my mouth, the seething
memory boils over in his shout:

"I'm hungry!" And immediately I feel
the undying hunger which this wretched creature
has long since ceased to feel, for which there is
no mitigating nourishment in nature.
He feeds on me. More and more hungrily!
And I'm less and less sufficient, for my part.

Now he, who would have been contented once
with any kind of food, demands my heart.

Translated by Clive Wilmer and George Gömöri

MARINA TSVETAEVA
Recommended by Vera Pavlova

Tsvetaeva's diaries are the stenographs of history—history that happens outside the window as well as history that happens behind the ribs. One cannot be separated from the other. Telegrams. Cardiograms.

ASSASSINATION ATTEMPT ON LENIN

Evening of the same day. My roommate, communist Zaks, bursting into the kitchen:

"And are you happy?"

I look down—not from shyness, of course: afraid to offend him. (Lenin has been shot. The White Army has entered the city, all the communists have been hanged, Zaks first among them.) Already I feel the generosity of the winning side.

"And you—are you very upset?"

"I?" (Tremble of shoulders.) "For us, Marxists, who don't recognize personal identity in history, this, in general terms, is not important—Lenin or someone else. It is you, the representatives of bourgeois culture," (new spasm), "with your Napoleons and your Caesars," (a devilish smile), "... but for us, us, us, you understand ... Today it is Lenin, and tomorrow it is—"

Offended on Lenin's behalf (!), I say nothing. Awkward pause. And then, quickly-quickly, he says:

"—Marina, I've got some sugar here, three-quarters of a pound, I don't need it; perhaps you would take it for your daughter?"

Daybook, Moscow, 1918–19

Translated by Ilya Kaminsky and Jean Valentine

César Vallejo
Recommended by Aleš Šteger

Sometimes poems are spiders—they catch readers in their webs, spin their invisible threads around us, leave us motionless and speechless. On the other hand, sometimes poems are bees—they feed us with nectar and awake in us a creative impulse, make us write. Whether the poem is a spider or a bee does not depend on the theme of the poem, but rather on the way the poem is structured, how currents of energy flow through it. I think "The Nine Monsters" of César Vallejo is a typical bee poem. Although it speaks about the tragic theme of human pain, it does so in an open form, with an inviting, long breath and an enigmatic, strong ending. Who, after having faced Vallejo's Minister of Health, doesn't feel the need to start to speak on his own?

The Nine Monsters

And, unfortunately,
pain grows in the world all the time,
grows thirty minutes a second, step by step,
and the nature of the pain, is twice the pain
and the condition of the martyrdom, carnivorous, voracious,
is twice the pain
and the function of the purest grass, twice
the pain
and the good of being, our dolor doubled.

Never, human men,
was there so much pain in the chest, in the lapel, in the wallet,
in the glass, in the butcher's shop, in arithmetic!
Never so much painful affection,
never did the distance charge so close,
never did the fire ever
play better its role of dead cold!
Never, Mr. Minister of Health, was health
more mortal,

did the migraine extract so much forehead from the forehead!
Did the cabinet have in its drawer, pain,
the heart, in its drawer, pain,
the lizard, in its drawer, pain.

Misfortune grows, brother men,
faster than the machine, at ten machines, and grows
with Rousseau's livestock, with our beards;
evil grows for reasons we know not
and is a flood with its own liquids,
its own mud and its own solid cloud!
Suffering inverts positions, it acts
in that the aqueous humor is vertical
to the pavement,
the eye is seen and this ear heard,
and this ear sounds nine strokes at the hour
of lightning, and nine guffaws
at the hour of wheat, and nine female sounds
at the hour of weeping, and nine canticles
at the hour of hunger, and nine thunderclaps
and nine lashes, minus a scream.

The pain grabs us, brother men,
from behind, in profile,
and drives us wild in the movies,
nails us to the gramophones,
unnails us in bed, falls perpendicularly
onto our tickets, our letters,
and it is very serious to suffer, one might pray . . .
For as a result
of the pain, there are some
who are born, others grow, others die,
and others who are born and do not die, others

who die, without having been born, and others
who neither are born nor die (the majority)
And likewise as a result
of suffering, I am sad
up to my head, and sadder down to my ankle,
from seeing bread, crucified, the turnip,
bloodied,
the onion, crying,
cereal, in general, flour,
salt, made dust, water, fleeing,
wine, an ecce-homo,
such pallid snow, such an ardent sun!
    How, human brothers,
not to tell you that I can no longer stand it and
can no longer stand so much drawer,
so much minute, so much
lizard and so much
inversion, so much distance and so much thirst for
    thirst!
Mr. Minister of Health: what to do?
Ah, unfortunately, human men,
there is, brothers, much too much to do.

Translated by Clayton Eshleman

EUGENIO MONTALE
Recommended by Adam Zagajewski

Again, it's not easy to choose just one poem by Montale. This poem, "Letter to Malvolio," a late one, is not really representative of nor typical of Montale. It's an angry poem, and the addressee of the anger is Pier Paolo Pasolini, who attacked the venerable older poet in a review for not being a writer committed to social causes. To remain a great poet in a poem filled with rage is remarkable. At the same time, this poem is certainly not the only occasion when a younger poet castigates an older one for not being in line with—with what, with the fad of the day? With the intellectual mood of the decade? With the ideas cherished by younger poets? Whoever wrote a better reply to such a challenge?

LETTER TO MALVOLIO

It was never a matter of my taking flight, Malvolio,
nor even some penchant of mine for sniffing out the worst
a thousand miles away. This is virtue
you possess, and one which I don't envy you either
since there's nothing in it for me.
                                                    No,
it was never a matter of taking flight,
simply a dignified
adoption of distance.

It was easy enough at the start
when the divisions were so marked—
horror on one side, and decency,
well, only an infinitesimal decency,
on the other. No, it wasn't so hard.

All it took was avoidance, fading away,
becoming invisible, maybe
being invisible. But later . . .

But later when the stables had emptied,
honor and indecency bonded in a single compact
established the permanent oxymoron
and the question was no longer one
of flight and refuge. It was the age
of the conceptual phocomele,
and the crooked was straight, and ridicule and silence
about everything else.

It was your age, and it isn't over.
With what dexterity you made your mishmash
of historical materialism and biblical pauperism,
pornography and redemption, disgust for the smell
of truffles, the money that came your way.
No, you're not wrong, Malvolio, the science of the heart
hasn't yet been born; each invents it as he likes.
But forget the flights now that one can hardly
look for hope in its own negation.
Let my motionless flight have the power to say Courage
to someone or to myself that the game is still on,
but the game is over for those who reject
distances and, like you, Malvolio, are always in a rush
since you know that tomorrow will be impossible
despite all your wiles.

Translated by William Arrowsmith

BERTOLT BRECHT
Recommended by Adam Zagajewski

Brecht produced hundreds of pages, most of them covered by the dialogues of his many plays. So was he seen by his contemporaries—as a great playwright. One wonders how will he fare in the river of time. There are voices in some of his poems in which he expressed himself stronger than in his theater. Both his theater and poetry are imbued with ideology. He loved being didactic; this was, he claimed, the vocation of literature, to teach. Brecht was a believer; his god was Karl Marx. But he was also an eminent writer, and his talent couldn't take this tension, couldn't always agree to this ideological imprisonment. "Of Poor B.B." is actually a rather early poem; here we see the poet in his pre-Marxist moment. The poet wants to be seen as cynical and sophisticated, and so he probably was. And yet there's poetry in this piece of lyric theater—He couldn't help it.

OF POOR B.B.

1
I, Bertolt Brecht, come from the black forests.
My mother carried me into the cities
When I was in her belly. And the chill of the forests
Will be in me till my dying day.

2
The asphalt city is my home. Furnished
From the outset with every sacramental perquisite:
With newspapers. And tobacco. And brandy.
Distrustful and idle and contented to the end.

3
I am friendly to people. I put on
A top hat because that's what they do.
I tell myself: They are animals with a particular smell.
And I tell myself: What of it, so am I.

4

In the morning I like to set a woman or two
In my empty rocking chairs
And I look at them insouciantly and I say to them:
In me you have someone on whom there is no relying.

5

Towards evening it's men I gather round around me
And we address our company as "gentlemen."
They park their feet on my table
And say: Things are looking up. And I don't ask: When?

6

In the gray pre-dawn the pine trees micturate
And their parasites, the birds, start to bawl.
At that hour I empty my glass in the city and throw away
My cigar end and worriedly go to sleep.

7

We have settled, a whimsical tribe,
In dwellings it pleased us to think of as indestructible
(In the same spirit we built the tall constructions on the
island of Manhattan
And the thin antennae that underwire the Atlantic Ocean).

8

Of these cities there will remain only what passed through them,
the wind.
The house makes glad the eater: he polishes it off.
We know we are provisional,
And that after us will come: really nothing worth mentioning.

9

In the coming earthquakes I trust
I will not let my Virginia go bitter on me,
I, Bertolt Brecht, removed to the asphalt cities
From the black forests in my mother in the early times.

Translated by Michael Hofmann

Miron Białoszewski
Recommended by Valzhyna Mort

Miron Białoszewski writes this exclamatory ode in a purposefully simple language. In fact, it is his own original language—the language he has created in order to celebrate the world of trivial objects in the ruins of the burned-down Warsaw.

And Even, Even If They Take Away the Stove
My Inexhaustible Ode to Joy

I have a stove
similar to a triumphal arch!

They take away my stove
similar to a triumphal arch! !

Give me back my stove
similar to a triumphal arch! ! !

They took it away.
What remains is
a gray
      naked
           hole

And this is enough for me;
gray naked hole
gray   naked   hole
graynakedhole.

Translated by Czesław Miłosz

ALEKSANDER WAT

Recommended by Valzhyna Mort

Aleksander Wat, the Polish poet whose admirers include Joseph Brodsky, Czesław Miłosz, and Tomaz Venclova, described himself as a person who managed to be who he ought to be, but always at the wrong time—a politician when he should have been a poet, and a poet when he should have been a politician; a communist when all decent people were anti-communists, and an anti-communist when everybody with a sense of reason became a communist; an avant-garde poet before Polish readers and poets developed an ear for experimentalism; and an already matured, serious poet when the scene started demanding experiments. He read Tolstoy and Proust when in prison, and in his poems, he celebrated life with his uncompromising, harsh wit.

BEFORE BREUGHEL THE ELDER

Work is a blessing.
I tell you that, I—professional sluggard!
Who slobbered in so many prisons! Fourteen!
And in so many hospitals! Ten! And innumerable inns!
Work is a blessing.
How else could we deal with the lava of fratricidal love
    towards fellow men?
With those storms of extermination of all by all?
With brutality, bottomless and measureless?
With the black and white era which does not want to
    end
endlessly repeating itself da capo like a record
forgotten on a turntable
spinning by itself?
Or perhaps someone invisible watches over the phono-
    graph? Horror!
How, if not for work, could we live in the paradise of
    social hygienists
who never soak their hands in blood without aseptic gloves?
Horror!

How else could we cope with death?
That Siamese sister of life
who grows together with it—in us, and is extinguished
    with it
and surely for that reason is ineffective.
And so we have to live without end,
without end. Horror!
How, if not for work, could we cope with ineffective
    death
(Do not scoff!)
which is like a sea,
where everyone is an Icarus, one of nearly three billion,
while besides so many things happen
and everything is equally unimportant, precisely,
    unimportant
although so difficult, so inhumanly difficult, so painful!
How then could we cope with all that?
Work is our rescue.
I tell you that—I, Breughel, the Elder (and I, for one,
your modest servant, Wat, Aleksander)—work is our
    rescue.

Translated by Czesław Miłosz

George Seferis

Recommended by Adam Zagajewski

In this case, in the case of Seferis, it's easy to choose—for me, this particular poem is the most beautiful in his oeuvre. There's something quite unique in the structure and action of "The King of Asine" (this king lives in human memory only because Homer devoted one line to him in the catalog of ships in *The Iliad*—and now also because Seferis offered him an entire poem). The uniqueness is that we, the readers, cannot be passive in receiving this poem. We have to become implicated in the plot. We have to believe in the premises of the poem, we have to be there, on the beach, in the kayak; we have to share the excitement and even the fatigue of the quest for the ancient king. And, if we're good readers, implicated, active, if our hearts beat along with the poem, we'll eventually recognize the presence of the king. The king will appear to us. So this is not a poem for the lukewarm.

"The King of Asine" also corresponds to what we always do when visiting old places, old towns, ruins: we desperately wish to experience a bit of the past that is just there, in front of our eyes but hopelessly absent. And yet it is there in this poem, and how! Seferis's poem is a magical formula, a spell that allows us to open the past again. We should travel with it.

The King of Asine

> Ἀσίνην τε ...
> —*The Iliad*

We looked all morning round the citadel
starting from the shaded side, there where the sea
green and without luster—breast of a slain peacock—
received us like time without an opening in it.
Veins of rock dropped down from high above,
twisted vines, naked, many-branched, coming alive
at the water's touch, while the eye following them
struggled to escape the tiresome rocking,
losing strength continually.

On the sunny side a long open beach
and the light striking diamonds on the huge walls.
No living thing, the wild doves gone
and the king of Asine, whom we've been trying to find for two years now,
unknown, forgotten by all, even by Homer,
only one word in the *Iliad* and that uncertain,
thrown here like the gold burial mask.
You touched it, remember its sound? Hollow in the light
like a dry jar in dug earth:
the same sound that our oars make in the sea.
The king of Asine a void under the mask
everywhere with us everywhere with us, under a name:
"'Ασίνην τε ... 'Ασίνην τε ..."
                    and his children statues
and his desires the fluttering of birds, and the wind
in the gaps between his thoughts, and his ships
anchored in a vanished port:
under the mask a void.

Behind the large eyes the curved lips the curls
carved in relief on the gold cover of our existence
a dark spot that you see traveling like a fish
in the dawn calm of the sea:
a void everywhere with us.
And the bird that flew away last winter
with a broken wing:
abode of life,
and the young woman who left to play
with the dogteeth of summer
and the soul that sought the lower world squeaking
and the country like a large plane-leaf swept along by the torrent of the sun
with the ancient monuments and the contemporary sorrow.

And the poet lingers, looking at the stones, and asks himself
does there really exist
among these ruined lines, edges, points, hollows, and curves
does there really exist
here where one meets the path of rain, wind, and ruin
does there exist the movement of the face, shape of the tenderness
of those who've shrunk so strangely in our lives,
those who remained the shadow of waves and thoughts with the sea's boundlessness
or perhaps no, nothing is left but the weight
the nostalgia for the weight of a living existence
there where we now remain unsubstantial, bending
like the branches of a terrible willow tree heaped in permanent despair
while the yellow current slowly carries down rushes uprooted in the mud
image of a form that the sentence to everlasting bitterness has turned to marble:
the poet a void.

Shieldbearer, the sun climbed warring,
and from the depths of the cave a startled bat
hit the light as an arrow hits a shield:
"'Ασίνην τε . . . 'Ασίνην τε . . ." Could be the king of Asine
we've been searching for so carefully on this acropolis
sometimes touching with our fingers his touch upon the stones.

Asine, summer 1938–Athens, January 1940

Translated by Edmund Keeley and Philip Sherrard

Nâzim Hikmet

Recommended by Nikola Madzirov

While they still search for a permanent place for Hikmet's bones, his flesh is long ago dissolved in the soil and feeds the plane-trees of vertical exile.

A Fable of Fables

We stand at the source,
the plane tree and I.
Our images reflect
off the river.
The water-dazzle
lights up the plane tree and me.

We stand at the source,
the plane tree, me, and the cat.
Our images reflect
off the river.
The water-dazzle
lights up the plane tree, me, and the cat.

We stand at the source,
the plane tree, me, the cat, and the sun.
Our images reflect
off the river.
The water-dazzle
lights up the plane tree, me, the cat, and the sun.

We stand at the source,
the plane tree, me, the cat, the sun, and our lives.
Our images reflect
off the river.
The water-dazzle
lights up the plane tree, me, the cat, the sun, and our lives.

We stand at the source.
The cat will be the first to go,
its image in the water will dissolve.
Then I will go,
my image in the water will dissolve.
Then the plane tree will go,
its image in the water will dissolve.
Then the river will go,
the sun alone remaining,
and then it, too, will go.

Translated by Randy Blasing and Mutlu Konuk Blasing

RAYMOND QUENEAU
Recommended by Valzhyna Mort

Raymond Queneau was a mathematician, scholar, poet, and a novelist who liked to hit poetic language on the head with a hammer of mischief and humor. The mathematical precision of his images works like a clock. "Poor Fellow" and "9" are sharp and passionately naughty.

POOR FELLOW

Toto has a goat's nose and the foot of a pig
He carries his socks
in a matchbox
and he combs his hair
with a hung-up paper cutter
If he gets dressed the walls turn gray
If he gets up the bed explodes
If he washes the water snorts
In his button-hole
he always has a button-hook

Poor fellow

from **TOWARD A POETIC ART**

9

This evening
what if I were to write a poem
for posterity?

helluva
nidea

it don't scare me
none
so

I'll tell 'em
shit and doubleshit
and doubledoubleshit

that'll fool
posterity
waiting for its poem

Yes but

Translated by Teo Savory

EDVARD KOCBEK
Recommended by Nikola Madzirov

"Prison is a shortage of space compensated by a surplus of time," wrote poet Joseph Brodsky about the narrow dark space, coming from the large extended Russia (Brodsky 1990). In his poetry, Edvard Kocbek poses moral and existential dilemmas, since for thirty-seven years he lived under surveillance of the secret police, his life written down by police officials in every intimate detail. His personal file, under the number 584, spanning from 1944 until his death in 1981, contains 4,268 pages of reports. Eventually he could no longer believe either the walls or his own hands.

In the poem "Microphone in the Wall" (Kravanja 1977), he writes: "My spirit talks without voice, / shouts and screams inaudibly"; in his poem "Hands" (Scammell and Taufer 2004), he writes: "I have lived between my two hands / as between two brigands." One of the most unknown, yet significant Eastern European poets, who was born to live in a small space, with a great faith that his cell could be disintegrated to openness, wrote in a quiet language: "my true revenge / is a poem."

LONGING FOR JAIL

> I was late for the most important
> spiritual exercises of my life,
> I am left without proof
> of my true value.
> Each jail is a treasury,
> a secret drawer, a jealous
> torture chamber, the most important stage
> of an executioner's asceticism before he is
> corrupted by a naked woman holding a knife.
> I miss the delight of that love,
> I would die easier if I had counted out
> the squares on the floor of my solitary cell
> and in my thoughts completed the transparent frescoes
> on the dusty pane,
> and gazed through the walls
> at the frontier posts of mankind.

Now, my cell, you have collapsed,
disintegrated to openness,
the world is no longer a world of redeeming cruelty,
it's only a sabbath yard.
You can test me no more,
I am no longer a figure for the Christmas crib,
for a puppet show or display of robots.
I am preparing myself for a different game—
look, I am turning into a little gray mouse,
my hiding places are all around,
tonight I shall sleep in the sleeve of a child
with no right hand, tomorrow I shall dream
in the echo of a shadow that sleeps after its voyage
through a fairy tale that has no end.

Translated by Michael Scammell and Veno Taufer

Vladimír Holan

Recommended by Adam Zagajewski

Holan has his readers in many countries, perhaps more of them and more ardent in their admiration than those of Jaroslav Seifert, whose work was crowned with the Nobel Prize. His poetry excels at producing unexpected images and metaphors, but it's not a poetry of fireworks just for the sake of fireworks. "Nothing for show," concludes Holan in his "Snow," and we believe him. We believe him even if we remember that poetry cannot totally renounce "show" on expression, on metaphors. This poem by Holan reads like a precise antithesis of Brecht's "Of Poor B.B.," which is all "for show." There are two movements in poetry—one toward theatricality, toward posing, toward trying different disguises, and the opposite one, a tendency to strip poems and their authors of (almost) any pretense. Holan's "Snow" definitely belongs to the latter category. It also bears witness to the years of hardship in his life when he was left with not many solaces except for poetry, his family, and the fact that, even if ostracized by the government and unable to publish his poetic work for fifteen years, he still lived in the very center of old Prague, one of the magical places of Europe.

Snow

The snow began to fall at midnight. And it's true
that the best place to sit is in the kitchen,
even if it's the kitchen of insomnia.
It's warm there, you fix some food, drink wine
and look out the window into the familiar eternity.
Why should you worry whether birth and death are only two points,
when life is not a straight line after all.
Why should you torture yourself staring at the calendar
and wondering how much is at stake.
And why should you admit you have no money
to buy Saskia a pair of slippers?
And why should you boast
that you suffer more than others.

Even if there were no silence on earth,
that snow would have dreamed it up.
You're alone. As few gestures as possible. Nothing for show.

Translated by C.G. Hanzlicek and Dana Hábová

Daniil Kharms

Recommended by Valzhyna Mort

Daniil Kharms, out of all Russian writers in the first half of the twentieth century, seems to have found the most original (and perhaps, the most Russian) language of everyday horror. Ordinary horror that happens to ordinary people. My main motivation in picking this poem is its substantial length. You'll see, you'll thank me for this ridiculous reasoning because you won't want this poem to end.

"Dear Nikandr Andreyevich ..."

Dear
    Nikandr Andreyevich,

I received your letter and understood right away that it was from you. First I thought, what if it's not from you, but as soon as I opened it I knew it was from you, but I almost thought that it wasn't from you. I am glad that you have long been married because when a person marries the one whom he wanted to marry that means he has achieved that which he wanted. And so I am very glad that you got married because when a man marries someone he wanted to marry that means that he got what he wanted. Yesterday I received your letter and right away I thought that this letter was from you, but then I thought it seemed that it wasn't from you, but I unsealed it and saw it was certainly from you. You did very well to write me. At first you didn't write to me and then suddenly you did write, although earlier, before you didn't write me for some time you also wrote to me. As soon as I received your letter I decided right away that it was from you and that's why I'm very glad that you had already married. Because if a man wants to get married then he must get married no matter what. That's why I am so very glad that you finally married precisely the one you wanted to marry. And you did very well to write me. I was overjoyed when I saw your letter and right away I thought it was from you. Although, to tell the truth, while I was opening it a thought flashed through my mind that it was not from you, but then in the end I decided that it was from you. Thanks for writing. I am grateful to you for this and very happy for you. Perhaps you can't imagine why I am so happy for you, but I'll tell you straight away that I am happy for you because, because you got married and married precisely the person you wanted to marry. And, you know, it is very good to marry precisely the person you want to marry because precisely then you get what you wanted. And that is precisely the reason that I am so happy for you. And I am also happy that you wrote me a letter. Even from afar I knew that the letter was from you, but when I took it in my hands I thought: And what if it's not from you? And then I thought: No, of course it is from you. I myself am opening the letter and at the same time thinking: From you or not from you? From you or not from you? And then, when I opened it I could clearly see that it was from you. I was overjoyed and decided I would also write you a letter. I have lots to tell you, but I literally don't have the time. What I had time to tell you, I have told you in this letter, and the rest I will write you later because now I have no time left at all. At the least it's good that you wrote me a letter. Now I know that you've long been married. I knew, too, from previous letters, that you got married, and now I see it again: It's completely true, you got married. And I am very happy that you got married and wrote me a letter. As soon as I saw your letter, I knew that you had got married again. Well, I thought, it's good that you got married again and wrote me a letter about it. Now write to me and tell me, who is your new wife and how did it all happen. Relay my greetings to your new wife.

Daniil Kharms
September and October 25, 1933

Translated by Matvei Yankelevich

CESARE PAVESE

Recommended by Valzhyna Mort

This is how you stop a moment and turn it into eternity. Cesare Pavese, Whitman's student in long lines, generous with adjectives (three in one line!), has everything under control here, just like the poem's breeze that carries "blue smoke without breaking it." In fact, everything is fixed in timelessness with the help of some adjective denoting color, texture, or distance from the poet's eye. Like a well-planned presentation, everything the poet touches with his word momentarily dampens, thus acquiring a flavor. The fruit "ready to fall at a touch" fall at his command. The line breaks are essential here. They slow us down, because a poem, just like Pavese's fruit, streets, houses, clouds, tobacco, alcohol, and women, needs time to steep and ripen. This slow ascension of prosaic sentences into a poem is supported by a generous use of repetition, and subtle, unexpected turns of a phrase.

GRAPPA IN SEPTEMBER

The mornings pass clear and deserted
on the river's banks, fogged over by dawn,
their green darkened, awaiting the sun.
In that last house, still damp, at the edge
of the field, they're selling tobacco, blackish,
juicy in flavor: its smoke is pale blue.
They also sell grappa, the color of water.

The moment has come when everything stops
to ripen. The trees in the distance are quiet,
growing darker and darker, concealing fruit
that would fall at a touch. The scattered clouds
are pulpy and ripe. On the distant boulevards,
houses are ripening beneath the mild sky.

This early you see only women. Women don't smoke
and don't drink, they know only to stop in the sun
to let their bodies grow warm, as if they were fruit.
The air's raw with this fog, you drink it in sips
like grappa, everything here has a flavor.
Even the river water has swallowed the banks
and steeps them below, in the sky. The streets
are like women, they grow ripe without moving.

This is the time when each person should pause
in the street to see how everything ripens.
There's even a breeze, it won't move the clouds,
but it's enough to carry the blue smoke
without breaking it: a new flavor passing. And tobacco
is best when steeped in some grappa. That's why the women
won't be the only ones enjoying the morning.

Translated by Geoffrey Brock

ANNA SWIR
Recommended by Nikola Madzirov

The scent of my father is in the sunlight that misses the flowerpots, in the dampness that sketches the atlases of the new worlds upon the walls, in the rust of tools used by his hands to fix the TV sets in half the town before New Year's Day, in the steam that was coming out of his skin after each bathing in the unheated house of my childhood, which is still cold whenever I return and leave like a loyal postman of doubts.

I WASH THE SHIRT

For the last time I wash the shirt
of my father who died.
The shirt smells of sweat. I remember
that sweat from my childhood,
so many years
I washed his shirts and underwear,
I dried them
at an iron stove in the workshop,
he would put them on unironed.

From among all the bodies in the world,
animal, human,
only one exuded that sweat.
I breathe it in
for the last time. Washing this shirt
I destroy it
forever.
Now
only paintings survive him
which smell of oils.

Soup for the Poor

Through the streets of Warsaw
kitchens for the poor are hauled.
The poor stand in lines,
they warm themselves by bonfires
which are lit for them
in the streets of Warsaw.

It is the First World War.
Mother put on a kerchief,
covered her face, went out
into the street to stand in line
for the soup for the poor.

Mother was afraid
that the janitor's wife would see her.
Mother after all was
the wife of an artist.

A Film about My Father

They show a film about my father,
in that film
father is quiet, it's I
who shout against his tragedy,
stutter, comically
gesticulate.

In the audience
are the art connoisseurs. Why
is that woman so worked up?
After all we know
who is truly great.
We drink vodka with the truly great.
Whoever heard of him?
She compares him to Norwid,
crazy female.

Translated by Czesław Miłosz and Leonard Nathan

Yannis Ritsos
Recommended by Nikola Madzirov

Each leaving is quiet, spectral, and motionless despite the dynamics of borders, epochs, and homes. For years, I have been living and writing in the huge white cube of silence with its black dots erased by time, as a restored wall of a prison. I was born near the summer nights of Yannis Ritsos. We were separated by many histories. Now we are captains of our own loneliness.

Immobility of the Voyage
(First Movement)

Enormous nocturnal steamers arrested in their lights—
the stewards, the porters, the automobiles, the naval guard,
valises made of leather, pasted with foreign stamps,
domestic baskets of reed or of wicker, a disconcerted goat,
long lingering farewells, up above the masts.

You heard neither voice nor sob.—Is it perhaps that you did not
    notice?
Everything was mute and spectral—motionless
in movement—phantoms of other epochs and countries.

The harbor is petrified in the perpetually moving lights,
within the reflections of the deep. The pier,
a prodigious pure white cube of silence
and the voyage is neither leave-taking nor a home-coming—an
    ethereal bridge
over names that are familiar and names that are unfamiliar. And
    on this bridge,
dressed in his white uniform, the youthful captain slowly paced.
    (or was it perhaps the moon?)

Translated by Rae Dalven

Czesław Miłosz

Recommended by Adam Zagajewski

Czesław Miłosz was a prolific poet who left many good and some great poems; I admire so many of them. "Elegy for N.N." interests me particularly maybe because it's an example of a poem written in the mode of discovery and surprise. Miłosz was a poet and a philosopher; he had a strong mind and strong opinions, and a few of his poems turned into megaphones for his ideas (for instance, his "Oeconomia Divina," a great, angry poem from the 1970s—but perhaps lending itself all too easily to a convenient paraphrase.) "Elegy for N.N." has all the ingredients of Miłosz's poetic universe, but when you read it, you seem to feel under your fingers how the poem grew under the poet's pen, in inspiration, in a daydream. We don't know why the woman standing in the center of this poem doesn't have a name; N. N. means "nomen nescio," or "I don't know the name." This is how police refer to the anonymous dead—and yet we have enough biographical information to know that the woman in question proudly owned a name. It can be that by withdrawing it Miłosz wanted to equate her symbolically with those victims of modern genocide who ended up having no name and no face, just a number.

Elegy for N. N.

Tell me if it is too far for you.
You could have run over the small waves of the Baltic
and past the fields of Denmark, past a beech wood
could have turned toward the ocean, and there, very soon
Labrador, white at this season.
And if you, who dreamed about a lonely island,
were frightened of cities and of lights flashing along the highway
you had a path straight through the wilderness
over blue-black, melting waters, with tracks of deer and caribou
as far as the Sierras and abandoned gold mines.
The Sacramento River could have led you
between hills overgrown with prickly oaks.
Then just a eucalyptus grove, and you had found me.

True, when the manzanita is in bloom
and the bay is clear on spring mornings
I think reluctantly of the house between the lakes
and of nets drawn in beneath the Lithuanian sky.
The bath cabin where you used to leave your dress
has changed forever into an abstract crystal.
Honey-like darkness is there, near the veranda,
and comic young owls, and the scent of leather.

How could one live at that time, I really can't say.
Styles and dresses flicker, indistinct,
not self-sufficient, tending toward a finale.
Does it matter that we long for things as they are in themselves?
The knowledge of fiery years has scorched the horses standing at the forge,
the little columns in the marketplace,
the wooden stairs and the wig of Mama Fliegeltaub.

We learned so much, this you know well:
how, gradually, what could not be taken away
is taken. People, countrysides.
And the heart does not die when one thinks it should,
we smile, there is tea and bread on the table.
And only remorse that we did not love
the poor ashes in Sachsenhausen
with absolute love, beyond human power.

You got used to new, wet winters,
to a villa where the blood of the German owner
was washed from the wall, and he never returned.
I too accepted but what was possible, cities and countries.
One cannot step twice into the same lake
on rotting alder leaves,
breaking a narrow sun-streak.

Guilt, yours and mine? Not a great guilt.
Secrets, yours and mine? Not great secrets.
Not when they bind the jaw with a kerchief, put a little cross
    between the fingers,
and somewhere a dog barks, and the first star flares up.

No, it was not because it was too far
you failed to visit me that day or night.
From year to year it grows in us until it takes hold,
I understood it as you did: indifference.

Berkeley, 1963

Translated by Czesław Miłosz and Lawrence Davis

EDMOND JABÈS

Recommended by Valzhyna Mort

"Mark the first page of the book with a red marker for in the beginning the wound is invisible," opens Edmond Jabès in his *The Book of Questions*. "Mirror and Scarf" is chosen from his *From the Book to the Book*. Jabès defines his genre as neither poetry nor prose. He claims he writes in the new genre, the book—the book that contains all the books of the universe, created and taken apart ("Whatever contains is itself contained," he concludes below). In the beginning of this book is not just a word, but a wound—the wound of an artist. Under his silk scarf, Mardohai Simhon carries a scar.

MIRROR AND SCARF

> *"We will gather images and images of images up till the last, which is blank. This one we will agree on."*
> —Reb Carasso

Mardohai Simhon claimed the silk scarf he wore around his neck was a mirror.

"Look," he said, "my head is separated from my body by a scarf. Who dares give me the lie if I say I walk with a knotted mirror under my chin?

"The scarf reflects a face, and you think it is of flesh.

"Night is the mirror. Day the scarf. Moon and sun reflected features. But my true face, brothers, where did I lose it?"

At his death, a large scar was discovered on his neck.

The meaning of this anecdote was discussed by the rabbis.

Reb Alphandery, in his authority as the oldest, spoke first.

"A double mirror," he said, "separates us from the Lord so that God sees Himself when trying to see us, and we, when trying to see Him, see only our own face."

"Is appearance no more than the reflections thrown back and forth by a set of mirrors?" asked Reb Ephraim. "You are no doubt alluding to the soul, Reb Alphandery, in which we see ourselves mirrored. But the body is the place of the soul, just as the mountain is the bed of the brook. The body has broken the mirror."

"The brook," continued Reb Alphandery, "sleeps on the summit. The brook's dream is of water, as is the brook. It flows for us. Our dreams extend us.

"Do you not remember this phrase of Reb Alsem's: 'We live out the dream of creation, which is God's dream. In the evening our own dreams snuggle down into it like sparrows in their nests.'

"And did not Reb Hames write: 'Birds of night, my dreams explore the immense dream of the sleeping universe.'"

"Are dreams the limpid discourse between the facets of a crystal block?" continued Reb Ephraim. "The world is of glass. You know it by its brilliance, night or day."

"The earth turns in a mirror. The earth turns in a scarf," replied Reb Alphandery.

"The scarf of a dandy with a nasty scar," said Reb Ephraim.

("*Words are inside breath, as the earth is inside time.*"
— Reb Mares)

And Yukel said:

"The bundle of the Wandering Jew contains the earth and more than one star."

"Whatever contains is itself contained," said Reb Mawas.

The story I told you, as well as the commentaries it inspired, will be recorded in the book of the eye. The ladder urges us beyond ourselves. Hence its importance. But in a void, where do we place it?

("*God is sculpted.*"
— Reb Moyal)

Translated by Rosmarie Waldrop

ORHAN VELI
Recommended by Valzhyna Mort

Orhan Veli is the bad boy of Turkish poetry. His humor is rude; his attitudes are vulgar and unapologetic. His poems are short, irresistible, and, let's admit it, perfect.

RUMORS

Who says
I've fallen for Süheylâ?
Who saw me, who
Kissing Eleni
On the sidewalk in the middle of the day?
And they say I took Melâhat
To Alemdar,
Is that so?
I'll tell you about it later,
But whose knee did I squeeze on the streetcar?
Supposedly, I've developed a taste for the fleshpots of Galata.
I drink, get drunk,
Then take myself there.
Forget about all these, guys,
Forget, forget about them.
I know what I'm doing.

And what about me
Supposedly putting Muallâ on a rowboat
And making her sing out loud, "My soul is yearning for you . . ."
In the middle of the harbor?

SPREAD OUT

She's spread out;
Her skirt pulled up slightly;
She's lifted her arm, one can see her armpits;
And with one hand she's holding her breast;
I know, she thinks nothing
Evil by it,
I know;
Neither do I;
But how can a person,
A person lie like this?

MY LEFT HAND

I got drunk
And thought of you,
My left hand
My awkward hand
My poor hand.

BAD BOY

You cut school,
You catch birds.
At the seaside
You speak to bad boys.
You draw dirty pictures on the walls.
Nothing major but
You'll turn my head too.
What a bad boy
You are.

Translated by Murat Nemet-Nejat

Paul Celan

Recommended by Adam Zagajewski

This is a very famous poem, so much so that its author suffered from too much publicity surrounding it. Every anthology claimed this poem. Many philosophical debates (having to do with the situation of art after Auschwitz) were wrapped around this poem. As far as I know, Celan never dismissed his poem, and when he kept it away from yet another anthology he only meant to give this poem some years of solitude, not to reject it. The genesis of the poem is mysterious: it's a very early poem by Celan, published first in a magazine in Bucharest (in Romanian, not German) under the title "Tango of Death" and with some central motifs owed to a poem by Immanuel Weissglas, Celan's close friend and fellow poet. All this mystery doesn't contradict one thing: it's a very great poem, which makes us wonder now and again how beauty and horror can cohabitate. This wonder is almost a part of the poem itself, and that the poem works well because of it—provided no ideological fervor, no partisan emotion distorts our reading.

DEATHFUGUE

Black milk of daybreak we drink it at evening
we drink it at midday and morning we drink it at night
we drink and we drink
we shovel a grave in the air where you won't lie too cramped
A man lives in the house he plays with his vipers he writes
he writes when it grows dark to Deutschland your golden hair
    Margareta
he writes it and steps out of doors and the stars are all sparkling he
    whistles his hounds to stay close
he whistles his Jews into rows has them shovel a grave in the ground
he commands us play up for the dance

Black milk of daybreak we drink you at night
we drink you at morning and midday we drink you at evening
we drink and we drink
A man lives in the house he plays with his vipers he writes
he writes when it grows dark to Deutschland your golden hair
    Margareta

Your ashen hair Shulamith we shovel a grave in the air
    where you won't lie too cramped

He shouts dig this earth deeper you lot there you others sing up
    and play
he grabs for the rod in his belt he swings it his eyes are so blue
stick your spades deeper you lot there you others play on for the
    dancing

Black milk of daybreak we drink you at night
we drink you at midday and morning we drink you at evening
we drink and we drink
a man lives in the house your goldenes Haar Margareta
your aschenes Haar Shulamith he plays with his vipers

He shouts play death more sweetly this Death is a master from
    Deutschland
he shouts scrape your strings darker you'll rise up as smoke to the sky
you'll then have a grave then in the clouds where you won't lie too
    cramped

Black milk of daybreak we drink you at night
we drink you at midday Death is a master aus Deutschland
we drink you at evening and morning we drink and we drink
this Death is ein Meister aus Deutschland his eye it is blue
he shoots you with shot made of lead shoots you level and true
a man lives in the house your goldenes Haar Margarete
he looses his hounds on us grants us a grave in the air
he plays with his vipers and daydreams der Tod ist ein Meister aus
    Deutschland

dein goldenes Haar Margarete
dein aschenes Haar Shulamith

Translated by John Felstiner

Anna Kamienska
Recommended by Valzhyna Mort

Anna Kamienska's poetry is the defense of art in the era of mass-production and cheap utilitarianism. Kamienska's poetic history is the history of her spiritual life, or as Adam Zagajewski puts it, "an honest evolution toward religious conversion." On November 1, 1971, she writes in her diary:

> "The idea of a poem about Job. The thing is beginning to grow in me. A contemporary Job. God who is silent. Present in every place and in various shapes—Satan. Pawel said to leave out the ending, it's artificially tacked on, that Job is given back all his goods. Then I thought, I'll do it the other way around, starting from that ending. From Job who is happy once again but already crushed, incapable of happiness, broken. Job's happiness. Job's second happiness."

THE RETURN OF JOB

Job didn't die
didn't throw himself under a train
didn't croak in a vacant lot
the chimney didn't spew him out
despair didn't finish him off
he arose from everything
from misery dirt
scabs loneliness

How much more authentic a dead Job would be
even after death shaking his fist at the God of pain
But Job survived
washed his body of blood sweat pus
and lay down in his own house again
New friends were already gathering
a new wife was breathing new love into his mouth
new children were growing up with soft hair

for Job to touch with his hands
new sheep donkeys oxen were bellowing
shaking new shackles in the stable
kneeling on straw

But happy Job didn't have the strength to be happy
afraid he'd betray happiness by a second happiness
afraid he'd betray life by a second life
Wouldn't it be better for you Job
to rot in a lost paradise with the dead
than to wait now for their nightly visit
they come in dreams they envy your life
Wouldn't it be better happy Job
to remain dirt since you are dirt
The pustules washed off your hands and face
ate through your heart and liver
You will die Job
Wouldn't it be better for you
to die with the others
in the same pain and mourning
than to depart from this new happiness
You walk in the dark
wrapped in darkness
among new people
useless as a pang of conscience
You suffered through pain
now suffer through happiness

And Job whispered stubbornly Lord Lord

THOSE WHO CARRY

Those who carry grand pianos
to the tenth floor wardrobes and coffins
the old man with a bundle of wood hobbling toward the horizon
the lady with a hump of nettles
the madwoman pushing her baby carriage
full of empty vodka bottles
they all will be raised up
like a seagull's feather like a dry leaf
like an eggshell a scrap of newspaper on the street

Blessed are those who carry
for they will be raised

I WAS BORN

I was born
and I died
I don't remember anything else
a green river perhaps
a green tree
green eyes
and about this so much ado
such regrets about this

Translated by David Curzon and Grażyna Drabik

Osip Mandelstam
Recommended by Adam Zagajewski

This is a short poem of a great force. Apparently it was written after Mandelstam—then on the road, fleeing the unsafe life in Kiev and heading for the south of Russia—learned of the execution of his fellow poet, Nicolay Gumilev, a member (like Mandelstam himself) of the (later very famous) Acmeist group of young poets. This happened in 1921. The poem, which bears the same year as Gumilev's execution, was probably written shortly after Mandelstam received this ominous news. The information of Gumilev's death meant more to him than a tragic end of a friend's life (as if this was not enough). It was for Mandelstam a terrible confirmation that the new Soviet civilization was going to be a criminal one. He hoped for a better world, but he was a sober observer (next to being an inspired poet, a poet of enormous metaphorical serendipity, and also a wonderful sense of humor). The night washing, under the starry sky, has in it something raw, cruel, and utterly beautiful.

I Was Washing in the Yard at Night

I was washing in the yard at night.
The firmament was brilliant with rude stars.
On an axe, the starlight looked like salt—
The barrel cooling, filled up to the brim.

The gates are tightly shut and locked
And the earth in conscience most severe.
No foundation is likely to be found
More pure than the truth of fresh linen.

Like a grain of salt, a star melts in the barrel,
And the water becomes even blacker—
Death more pure, more salty grief,
And the earth more frightening, more truthful.

Translated by Ilya Bernstein

VASKO POPA
Recommended by Nikola Madzirov

Vasko Popa: the poet who locked the essence of myth and folklore into a little box and allowed just a glance through the keyhole. I have never been to the village of my ancestors, who had to leave it because of the Balkan Wars almost a century ago. They say weeds live in the houses now, with buried toys and lachrymatories. Popa opens his poem with a touch—with a hug—and finishes it with a touch upon the cheek. Yet he remains a dreamer.

IN THE VILLAGE OF MY ANCESTORS

Someone embraces me
Someone looks at me with the eyes of a wolf
Someone takes off his hat
So I can see him better

Everyone asks me
Do you know how I'm related to you

Unknown old men and women
Appropriate the names
Of young men and women from my memory

I ask one of them
Tell me for God's sake
Is George the Wolf still living

That's me he answers
With a voice from the next world

I touch his cheek with my hand
And beg him with my eyes
To tell me if I'm living too

Translated by Charles Simic

VESNA PARUN
Recommended by Nikola Madzirov

I was about ten years old when my grandfather passed away. All that I can remember is his firm embrace of the contrabass and the smell of mountain tea that used to move the mountains into our room whenever he came back from picking herbs. He was born on the road, while his parents were escaping during the Balkan Wars, and since then, he served in many armies. He spent both World Wars here on the Balkans, and he changed many countries without having to travel, but I never perceived him as one who would kill. He was sitting in front of the house watching the leaves fall down, like soldiers, as Ungaretti would put it.

MY GRANDFATHER

My grandfather sits in front of the house and leaves fall.
    He looks at the figs that dry on the stone,
while the sun, very orange, vanishes behind the small vineyards
    I remember from childhood.

The voice of my grandfather is golden, like the melody of an old clock,
and his dialect is rich, filled with restlessness.
The legend of "Seven Lean Years" follows right after the "Our Father," short and
eternal.

One day, there was no more fishing.
Now, there is war.
The enemy surrounds the port for miles around.
The whole tiny island trembles in eclipse.
All her sons disappeared in search of war wages—
a long time ago.
Canada,
Australia . . .
They'll board them next for Japan.
It's possible they'll stay forever with their heads among the bamboo.
This is the second winter that they've marched nonstop.
Even the fish sound gloomy in their chase.

One grandson is handsome and good, yet, we'll find him in the snow one day
when the mountains are tired.

The girls sing as they prepare the picnic soup.
The children squat on the floor, very frightened
of the boots of the elegant old man.
One mother thinks of the sons and father who became a Malayan.

Strange, how this family has been scattered over four continents.
These big brawny people sound like children in their letters.

My grandfather stares at the red sun in the vineyard,
worn to silence, because death approaches the old fisherman of the sea.
Foreign greed; strange hunger. Freedom is a bit of breadcrust.

Ah, tell the earth that watermills should run faster!
A storm took the leaves away; whatever's right shall be.
So, the young boys die, and the old men warm up their sorrows,
                                        staring at the horizon.

Translated by Ivana Spalatin and Daniela Gioseffi

YVES BONNEFOY
Recommended by Valzhyna Mort

Yves Bonnefoy's poems turn their luminous attention to the elemental things of the everyday. His poetic desire is not to replace God, but to discover and illuminate the simple and true order of life—celebrate earthly, mortal presences.

PLACE OF THE SALAMANDER

The startled salamander freezes
And feigns death.
This is the first step of consciousness among the stones,
The purest myth,
A great fire passed through, which is spirit.

The salamander was halfway up
The wall, in the light from our windows.
Its gaze was merely a stone,
But I saw its heart beat eternal.

O my accomplice and my thought, allegory
Of all that is pure,
How I love that which clasps to its silence thus
The single force of joy.

How I love that which gives itself to the stars by the inert
Mass of its whole body,
How I love that which awaits the hour of its victory
And holds its breath and clings to the ground.

Translated by Galway Kinnell and Richard Pevear

MIROSLAV HOLUB
Recommended by Valzhyna Mort

Laboratory-clean poems of the immunologist and poet Miroslav Holub have been described as "mathematics with blood in it" (Breslin 1997). "Half a Hedgehog" is a prayer to the God of Logic. I've picked this poem for its grim wit, for its refusal of poetical embellishment, and for its sinister re-appropriation of Cesare Pavese's "death will come . . ." line.

HALF A HEDGEHOG

The rear half had been run over,
leaving the head and thorax
and the front legs of the hedgehog shape.

A scream from a cramped-open
jaw. The scream of the mute is
more horrible than the silence after a flood,
when even black swans float
belly upwards.

And even if some hedgehog doctor were
to be found in a hollow trunk or under the leaves
in a beechwood there'd be no hope
for that mere half on Road E12.

In the name of logic,
in the name of the theory of pain,
in the name of the hedgehog god the father, the son
and the holy ghost amen,
in the name of games and unripe raspberries,
in the name of tumbling streams of love
ever different and ever bloody,
in the name of the roots which overgrow
the heads of aborted foetuses,

in the name of satanic beauty,
in the name of skin bearing human likeness,
in the name of all halves
and double helices, of purines
and pyrimidines

we tried to run over
the hedgehog's head with the front wheel.

And it was like guiding a lunar module
from a planetary distance,
from a control centre seized
by cataleptic sleep.

And the mission failed. I got out
and found a heavy piece of brick.
Half the hedgehog continued screaming. And now
the scream turned into speech,

prepared by
the vaults of our tombs:
Then death will come and it will have your eyes.

Translated by Ewald Osers

WISŁAWA SZYMBORSKA
Recommended by Adam Zagajewski

An exquisite poem this is, an elegy operating in the most discreet way. We'll never know who's being elegized here, though the poet's friends, if asked, could tell us who it was. The loss is seen through the figure of a cat left alone in the apartment that once had an important human presence. It's only through negation, through suggestion, that the poet conveys her sorrow; the cat, an animal that doesn't have much of a reputation as far as fidelity is concerned (that is reserved for dogs), is chosen to represent the bereavement. The cat figure corresponds very well to the psychological and philosophical profile of the poet as it emerges from Szymborska's oeuvre—an autonomous person, someone who cherishes freedom, an independent, ironic mind of a late humanist. Yet independent, ironic people fall in love, too, and are sometimes left mourning and despairing. A cat can help then, at least within a poem: cats are walking and leaping symbols of freedom, but they attract our love all the same.

CAT IN AN EMPTY APARTMENT

Die—you can't do that to a cat.
Since what can a cat do
in an empty apartment?
Climb the walls?
Rub up against the furniture?
Nothing seems different here,
but nothing is the same.
Nothing has been moved,
but there's more space.
And at nighttime no lamps are lit.

Footsteps on the staircase,
but they're new ones.
The hand that puts fish on the saucer
has changed, too.

Something doesn't start
at its usual time.
Something doesn't happen
as it should.
Someone was always, always here,
then suddenly disappeared,
and stubbornly stays disappeared.

Every closet has been examined.
Every shelf has been explored.
Excavations under the carpet turned up nothing.
A commandment was even broken:
papers scattered everywhere.
What remains to be done.
Just sleep and wait.

Just wait till he turns up,
just let him show his face.
Will he ever get a lesson
on what not to do to a cat.
Sidle towards him
as if unwilling
and ever so slow
on visibly offended paws,
and no leaps or squeals at least to start.

Translated by Stanisław Barańczak and Clare Cavanagh

NINA CASSIAN
Recommended by Valzhyna Mort

All poetry reminds us of our mortality, but when this reminder is delivered by Nina Cassian, we, having abandoned all hope, need not abandon our humor and self-deprecation.

TEMPTATION

Call yourself alive? Look, I promise you
that for the first time you'll feel your pores opening
like fish mouths, and you'll actually be able to hear
your blood surging through all those lanes,
and you'll feel light gliding across the cornea
like the train of a dress. For the first time
you'll be aware of gravity
like a thorn in your heel,
and your shoulder blades will ache for want of wings.
Call yourself alive? I promise you
you'll be deafened by dust falling on the furniture,
you'll feel your eyebrows turning to two gashes,
and every memory you have—will begin
at Genesis.

FAIRYTALE

—Why is this that the ugliest of the ugly,
the most hideous of the hideous—wants to be called Prince Charming?
—But, answered the Princess, what befits a disguise?
What if inside that scabby toad there lies bewitched
the wonderful Prince himself?
That's a risk I dare not take.

And the Princess kissed his warts
and took him to bed.
And the scabby toad croaked—
satisfied.

Us Two

My God, what a dream I had:
the two of us, more passionate than ever,
making love like the first couple on earth . . .
—and we were so beautiful, naked and wild,
and both dead.

Translated by Andrea Deletant and Brenda Walker

Zbigniew Herbert
Recommended by Adam Zagajewski

When it comes to deciding which poem by Herbert to propose, the choice is difficult, but perhaps less so than in the case of Czesław Miłosz, for instance, who tried different voices, different dictions. Herbert's work is more consolidated (this is not, for me, a value judgment, just an observation). There are degrees and tonalities in Herbert's poetry as well; there's a pole of humor and a pole of tragic seriousness (the latter can be seen in "The Envoy of Mr. Cogito"). "The Seventh Angel" is on the lighter side. Herbert invents here an angel, Shemkel, who's like the warmhearted village priests in older Italian movies (these were good times; priests have a different image now). Shemkel tries to help sinners, and his reputation is pretty bad—everyone knows that, compared to other angels, he's a suspect character. Shemkel: "black nervous / in his old threadbare nimbus." Unlike majestic angels floating in the poems of some other poets, Shemkel doesn't scare us—Shemkel is a nice guy. Herbert's irony is life-giving, not dry, and as theoretical as that in many postmodern books.

The Seventh Angel

The seventh angel
is completely different
even his name is different
Shemkel

he is no Gabriel
the aureate
upholder of the throne
and baldachin

and he's no Raphael
tuner of choirs

and he's also no
Azrael
planet-driver

surveyor of infinity
perfect exponent of theoretical physics

Shemkel
is black and nervous
and has been fined many times
for illegal import of sinners

between the abyss
and the heavens
without a rest his feet go pit-a-pat

his sense of dignity is non-existent
and they only keep him in the squad
out of consideration for the number seven

but he is not like the others

not like the hetman of the hosts
Michael
all scales and feathery plumes

nor like Azrafael
interior decorator of the universe
warden of its luxuriant vegetation
his wings shimmering like two oak trees

not even like
Dedrael
apologist and cabalist

Shemkel Shemkel
—the angels complain
why are you not perfect

the Byzantine artists
when they paint all seven
reproduce Shemkel
just like the rest

because they suppose
they might lapse into heresy
if they were to portray him
just as he is
black nervous
in his old threadbare nimbus

Translated by Czesław Miłosz and Peter Dale Scott

SHAMSHAD ABDULLAEV
Recommended by Valzhyna Mort

Shamshad Abdullaev from the Fergana Valley in Uzbekistan is not Russian, but his poetic language of choice is. "Summer, Landscape" opens with short sentences, which lead to the central image that occupies most of the poem's body: the eye of a half-naked butcher follows a stream of the sheep's blood, sees it turn into a song (it is the throat that's cut!) and finally answers the sheep's blood with his own stream of sweat cutting his nipple in two. This image works on the reader as a spell. By the time we come to the two final questions and the answer, we are already poem-struck, frozen in the heat of this Central Asian landscape.

SUMMER, LANDSCAPE

Sun-struck, a boy on a red-hot square, light
and shadow. Beads
in the hand of an old woman. A bird
with lilac feathers screams, flies up, and from afar
whispers its quiet curse. It's sunny and stuffy, as if at this moment
a young half-naked butcher, holding
his breath, were waiting for blood
to stream by itself—in the paroxysm of impatient
sacrifice—from the throat of a black sheep
like a song of praise for the Southern sun; and
later, a dark trickle (sweat) would cut
a well-defined male nipple. But
who would move us?
Who would break the spell?
The earth, your lips, a red bird.

Translated by Valzhyna Mort

HANS MAGNUS ENZENSBERGER
Recommended by Nikola Madzirov

When the poet keeps silent, he doesn't conceal. He says I die, and only the seed in a closed hand trusts him.

FURTHER REASONS WHY POETS DO NOT TELL THE TRUTH

Because the moment
when the word *happy*
is pronounced
never is the moment of happiness.
Because the thirsty man
does not give mouth to his thirst.
Because *proletariat* is a word
which will not pass the lips of the proletariat.
Because he who despairs
does not feel like saying:
"I am desperate."
Because orgasm and *orgasm*
are worlds apart.
Because the dying man,
far from proclaiming:
"I die," only utters
a faint rattle,
which we fail to comprehend.
Because it is the living
who batter the ears of the dead
with their atrocities.
Because words come always
too late or too soon.
Because it is someone else,
always someone else,
who does the talking,

and because he
who is being talked about,
keeps his silence.

Translated by Michael Hamburger

DANE ZAJC
Recommended by Nikola Madzirov

Writing about time is pouring letters through the narrow opening of the hourglass. "What, then, is time? If no one asks me, I know what it is," says St. Augustine in his *Confessions*. Amichai writes: "A man doesn't have time in his life to have time for everything." Dane Zajc talks about the time when instead of turning from earth into dust, one would turn from ice into vapor, would melt with the sounds uttered when time was not so cruel, when language and words could not stop breathing. What is time, then, what is your time?

YOUR TIME

Time comes when there is no more time.
A footstep halts, cannot go ahead.
Eyes look at themselves,
with a gaze full of reproach.
Where have you brought me, they say.
Why are you stiff with fear.
Why locked in icy immobility.

Time comes when time is cruel.
Inexorable.
The lips frozen.
Unstirring.
And the tongue, dry from cognition,
plunges into the cavity of
the throat.

Time when you halt.
When you are the ice of your own self.
Your time.

Translated by Sonja Kravanja and Dane Zajc

Vytautas P. Bložė
Recommended by Eugenijus Ališanka

Vytautas P. Bložė is one of the most important authors for many Lithuanian poets of the younger generation. He has made a big impact on my writing as well. In fact, he writes not single poems but cycles and books, which is why it is difficult to select a single poem. What I like about his poetry is that you can plunge into it and swim endlessly, getting to know more and more about life and poetry. This poem, as the reader might notice, is from a big cycle as well. Bložė starts with a paraphrase of a famous fairytale—a Prince kisses the frog. This frog, however, turns into not a beautiful girl into an amazing picture of life, which is not a fairy tale, but it could use one. I think this phenomenon is the key to poetry (as is a key to a forbidden room in most of fairy tales), and Bložė has found it. You need the frog, but you do not need to kiss it. This is the essence of poetry.

III. (from *Preludes*)

I will take a frog for a wife
and will live in an old swamp where smoke
floats along the ground, where stars
twinkle high above: my days
have scattered in the forest, and wind
carries them, scarred and with cut
roots or sewed together with a thick needle
and the stitched thread
of waxed memories: where is the middle
of this story? Where is the orphan girl? A swing
rocks under a branch in the yard. Where is the green
land of the forest? It stopped
near the stream because there was
no bridge and trees
stood without coming together, only occasionally
wading across the shallow places or in winter
when they brought the ice. I will take
a frog for a wife, where spider webs

dry as they curl across my forehead.
Where the forest stars fall
into coffins in the tops of the oak trees
into coffins in the tops of the oak trees
into coffins in the tops of the oak trees where those
without countries are buried. Where their black
hands grew, holding
a cross, rain, and the falling
snow of the trees. Two large
tears flow. Where
are the deer? At the bottom of the creek
their shirts dry
where the chalk of the manor was burned out. The master
was at war in Hungary and brought back
a leg of a foreign tree: the maid
tore the feathers of screeching birds. Where did they lay
the first dog, the first cry
where is the bark of the birch? Where scattered
days sleep among the mosses
with the rabbits: with eyes open

and lips firmly clenched: I find only part
of a smile in the left pocket. Where are the two
violets from the old letter? Beyond the town's
fence the hornpipes of the blind
played as the frog
danced on the floor: like a princess on my palm
the small forest frog, brought to me by the stork
I will live until my death and will find
great truth in bread, that I crumbled
for the birds who had no nests
as I walked in the forests: once again
burial mounds will rise and the stones

will fall, and someone will run to the other side
splashing time. Where my girl
is sleeping, where my girl
is sleeping for a thousand years

and the bridge is burned
and the crow holds in its beak
her pecked out eyes

Translated by Jonas Zdanys

TOMAS TRANSTRÖMER
Recommended by Aleš Šteger

I read the poem "Schubertiana" by Tomas Tranströmer as a religious act without religion. It is a poem of hope, a very intimate one, capable of creating intimacy through a wide fresco of images of big distances, modern technology, a metropolis, and our everyday lives as inhabitants of cities whose complexities are beyond imagination. Tranströmer's voice is unique, giving firm and extremely exact measures to what seems immeasurable: our contemporary nature.

SCHUBERTIANA

1

In the evening darkness in a place outside New York, a viewpoint where one single glance will encompass the homes of eight million people.

The giant city becomes a long shimmering drift, a spiral galaxy seen from the side.

Within the galaxy coffee cups are pushed across the counter, the shop windows beg from passersby, a flurry of shoes leave no prints.

The climbing fire escapes, elevator doors glide shut, behind police-locked doors a perpetual seethe of voices.

Slouched bodies doze in subway cars, the hurtling catacombs.

I know too—without statistics—that right now Schubert is being played in a room over there and that for someone the notes are more real than anything else.

2

The endless expanses of the human brain are crumpled to the size of a fist.

In April the swallow returns to last year's nest under the guttering of this very barn in this very parish.

She flies from Transvaal, passes the equator, flies for six weeks over two continents, makes for precisely this vanishing dot in the land-mass.

And the man who catches the signals from a whole life in a few ordinary chords for five strings,

who makes a river flow through the eye of a needle,

is a stout young gentleman from Vienna known to his friends as "The Mushroom,"
   who slept with his glasses on
and stood at his writing desk punctually in the morning.
And then the wonderful centipedes of his manuscript were set in motion.

3

The string quintet is playing. I walk home through warm forests with the ground
   springy under me,
curl up like an embryo, fall asleep, roll weightless into the future, suddenly feel
   that the plants have thoughts.

4

So much we have to trust, simply to live through our daily day without sinking
   through the earth!
Trust the piled snow clinging to the mountain slope above the village.
Trust the promises of silence and the smile of understanding, trust that the
   accident telegram isn't for us and that the sudden axe-blow from within
   won't come.
Trust the axles that carry us on the highway in the middle of the three hundred
   times life-size bee-swarm of steel.
But none of this is really worth our confidence.
The five strings say we can trust something else. And they keep us company part
   of the way.
As when the time-switch clicks off in the stairwell and the fingers—trustingly—
   follow the blind handrail that finds its way in the darkness.

5

We squeeze together at the piano and play with four hands in F minor, two
   coachmen on the same coach, it looks a little ridiculous.
The hands seem to be moving resonant weights to and fro, as if we were tampering
   with the counterweights
in an effort to disturb the great scale arm's terrible balance: joy and suffering
   weighing exactly the same.

Annie said, "This music is so heroic," and she's right.
But those whose eyes enviously follow men of action, who secretly despise
  themselves for not being murderers,
don't recognize themselves here,
and the many who buy and sell people and believe that everyone can be bought,
  don't recognize themselves here.
Not their music. The long melody that remains itself in all its transformations,
  sometimes glittering and pliant, sometimes rugged and strong, snail track
  and steel wire.
The perpetual humming that follows us—now—
up
the depths.

Translated by Robin Fulton

NORA IUGA
Recommended by Valzhyna Mort

To write about Nora Iuga means to write a love letter. Words like magnificent, beautiful, as well as surrealism, oneiric, and balkanism spring up, but they are only handkerchiefs Iuga holds up to her mouth when clearing up her throat. Her eroticism—her Cupid—walks blindfolded, crashing into the walls of pain, desire, lust, and finally a page where a poem is being born. *Caprices* is an erotic dream of a seventy-year-old woman: magnificent, beautiful, surreal.

from "CAPRICES"

13

then the phone rang
a white horse appeared
and ate from my palm
my hand crossed the red sea
it reached the promised land
stone by stone my way is clear
stone by stone my flesh becomes thinner
there was a character who came out of nowhere
the very mouth of my beloved
today I crushed a hard black beetle
that looked so much
like Else Lasker-Schüler

14

why don't you want to believe
that at the moment of nightfall
your love awakens
that an endless transport of words rattles into motion
from an abandoned train station
the sky has a scaly belly
and when it shakes itself snowflakes fall
I'd like my thoughts to arrive in the world

incarnated as a man
I'd like an army-green tarpaulin
to throw over this car
that sputters clatters
and jolts me

15

She told me to dye my hair
and get it cut
I want to stay an untamed creature
as in childhood
when trees were god's lungs
and stars the yellow eyes of a terrified beast

I step on roots and believe
they're my lover's arms
I step on stones and imagine they're his knees
soon I'll enter the song of songs
and become the laughing stock of this
petty world this warren of spies

16

I don't know how
he showed up just like a plumber
unclogged my words
and made them flow
maybe there are cycles
every three years or so
when faucets must have their washers replaced
during the glorious month of October
then in a blind waltz I permit myself to lead
to most profitable places

20

let me be with my head under the pillow
I don't want to listen to the cassette tapes
let me alone in my sleep
in my train station
where two bodies
can pass by
without bumping into each other

22

I don't know why there came to mind
the wardrobe with five padlocks
above each padlock a blue star
and below a useless horizontal key slot

at night on the train I study
my hand with its five fingers
when I feel cold
and the railroad car is empty

23

how easy it is to go on living
without your body
when I can invent it
for any occasion
all these silent conversations
spread on paper
like butter on a slice of bread
my little drug
I recognize that I deceive myself
but I can't always be aware
as along my way I crush
the swallow's nestling

24

look my monologue has broken off
I don't know what the problem might be
perhaps the too blinding light
or a pull on my brain
toward another region
the way little beggars come
and tug on your sleeve
all these small coins
falling into your neurons
as if into a hi-fi speaker
I feel so estranged
from the poet I've been reading
the water dripping in the bathtub
accompanies my silence
like cicadas once upon a time

25

for a long time I'll find it impossible
to make the rounds of eden
if you fail to invent some pretext
to telephone me
a plump round friday appears
a tunnel appears
like a huge vagina
quietly I play with the tassels
and I'm as well-behaved
as a cloth doll
left behind on a park bench

26

how many tender gestures
does a woman need
to fall in love
twenty leagues under the sea
the cabin door of the former schooner
is ready to fall open
fish and people
the living and the dead
a continuous rocking
like the great explorations of sex

27

how I long never to be raised again
from this page
to remain buried in it
for eternity
I feel your breath
in the invisible pores of the paper
and it's as if I can hear caesar whispering
from the cliffs above the great canyon
"I tried to warm the gods
with my regard"

Translated by Adam J. Sorkin with Ioana Ieronim

Nichita Stănescu

Recommended by Nikola Madzirov

One of Stănescu's poem-dialogues about the soldier and the bird came to me when I was killing all my promises while in the army, and ever since then his words have been coming to me in waves like a child left in a swinging cradle. His poems written in the language of seeds cross my threshold like a shadow and an apple of pure presence. I locked my uniform in the freezer; his poetry remained my weeping eye of the hand.

The Airplane Dance

The dance moved in circles, with airplanes:
some golden,
            some silver.

They went like this: a half circle
on the left side, going up
then down, over the roofs
. . . then up, on the right
golden, silver.

How they spun as they fell
          golden, silver . . .

After that a neighbor's house was gone
and the house on the corner
and the house next door . . .

And I was amazed
and shook my head:
look, there's no house! . . .
look, there's no house! . . .
look, there's no house! . . .

The Fifth Elegy

The temptation of the real

I was never angry with apples
for being apples, with leaves for being leaves,
with shadow for being shadow, with birds for being birds.
But apples, leaves, shadows, birds,
all of a sudden, were angry with me.
See me taken before the court of leaves,
the court of shadows, apples, birds,
round courts, flying courts,
courts cool and thin.
See me condemned for ignorance,
boredom, disquiet,
stasis.
Sentences written in the language of seeds.
Indictments sealed
with the innards of birds,
cool, ashen atonements, chosen for me.
I rise, head uncovered,
and I try to understand what I deserve
for stupidity . . .
and I cannot, I cannot understand
anything,
and this state itself
grows angry with me
and condemns me, in a way impossible to understand,
to a perpetual waiting,
to harmonize meanings with themselves
until they take the form of apples, leaves,
shadows,
birds.

Translated by Sean Cotter

Vlada Urošević
Recommended by Nikola Madzirov

There are two poems in Macedonian poetry entitled "Fear" that I often reread without the fear that I may learn them by heart—one is by Mihail Rendzov, and the other is by Vlada Urošević. One has a structure as a house on a hill, the other as a gallery of dreams. In a ritual rhythm come the images and silences in this poem, which in the end knit together into the trembling sound of the violin through the ancient naturalness of metamorphosis. Since the times of the canonized communist poetics of socrealism, Urošević brought to these spaces the half-dream of Borges, the phantasmagoric alertness of Michaux, the psychic automatism of Breton. Now one can calmly dream without fearing the sentence of time and long-sleeping ideology.

Fear

The hearing is held outside without many attorneys.
The crime has not been defined, the defendant still absent.
The first one to approach will accept the code of silence.
The shadows will approach and surround him.

There is a street outside which ends with a high wall and no entrance.
There are black jugglers in slimy carriages.
There are lost children carrying toys of lime.
There are gossip-mongers with mouths full of ashes.

Someone tries to unlock the lock of night.
The key slips from his hands and becomes a violin bow.
Violins of glass tremble in the arms of clumsy musicians.
The sheets of music are written over with the sentence.

Translated by Zoran Ančevski

GENNADY AYGI

Recommended by Valzhyna Mort

A poet of linguistic subtlety and bright silence, Gennady Aygi is playful without any ironies. His melancholy is whimsical. Mortal people and their immortal furniture are related not by blood, but by subtle movements connecting limbs and objects into one family. The temporality of "life in the form of people" is balanced by the permanence of "relatives" who stay at home while people leave for prisons and hospitals—for instance, not even the piano itself, but the patches of light on the piano that make it alive, and hint at of what might as well be: a cognitive illumination of the inanimate object.

PEOPLE

So many nights
the lines of chairs, frames, bureaus,
I have seen off with movements
of my arms and shoulders
on their regular

and unknown paths.

I didn't notice
how this happens too with people.
I must admit: when I talk to them,
I imagine my finger measuring

the lines of their eyebrows.

And they were everywhere,
so that I did not forget   ·
about life in the form of people,

and there were weeks and years
to say goodbye to them,

and there was the idea of thinking
so that I knew
the patches of light on their pianos
had relatives

in hospitals and prisons.

Translated by Sarah Valentine

VÉNUS KHOURY-GHATA

Recommended by Valzhyna Mort

A poet of exquisite imagination, Vénus Khoury-Ghata was born in Lebanon and resides in France, writing in French. Her poems are the fairytales of pain; told with surreal, sensual images. I believe there's something for all of us in this poem here.

from EARLY CHILDHOOD (excerpts)

My mother would lose herself in the puffing movements of her broom
battling the sand which she called desert
the dampness she called crumbled water
swamp

remote from the world her sweeper's hands
exhumed invisible corpses
pursued the least foundering of the wind
the slightest stain of darkness
she swept with such self-abnegation
and burst out laughing in the worst storm
for fear of appearing ill-tempered

Mother you were so modest
you took no credit for the wind which blew just for your arms as they swept.

[...]

We had explained our despair to the thorn bush and the juniper
our only cousins in that foreign language
we had cried on the shoulder of the pomegranate tree which bled on our doorstep
    every month

We had asked for an audience with the forest
and provided the testimony of two blackbirds who had seen us
    write the word "goat" in both directions
we had vanquished the alphabet

Our shoemaker spoke Sanskrit
the priest and the stream spoke Latin

We were blamed for our ignorance of ornithology
although we knew every star's name, and its precise punctuation on the sky's page.

[...]

I write Mother
and an old woman rises in the uncertainty of evening
slips into a wedding dress
stands on tiptoe on her windowsill
calls out to the hostile city
addresses the haughty tribe of streetlights
bares her chest to the clocks
shows them the precise site of her sorrow
disrobes gently for fear of creasing her wrinkles
and unsettling the air

My mother had her own way of undressing
as one would strip the medals from a disgraced general

A cold odor is in my mother's pockets
and three pebbles to break summer's windows
my mother's dress had drunk all November's snow
dead birds' cries had ripped holes in her hem

She chases them from her unconscious arms
insults them with the muteness of words
and the absence of echoes
within her walls knocked over
from within

It sometimes happens that despite the air's vigilance my mother gets up
arms herself with a spade
turns over great shovelfuls of earth which cover her
arousing the anger of taciturn neighbors who've turned their backs on the clocks
and broken off all correspondence with the grass
her chilled puffing and panting breaks through the soil down to that room
where, for lack of sun, she makes her knees shine and her tears sparkle.

[. . .]

Tired of drying a dead man's muddy tears under glass
she turned toward her garden
stanched the sweat of the pomegranate tree
cleaned up the lime tree's droppings

The evening which blued her doorway delivered her up to the wrath of nettles
which reclaimed their share of her compassion and shade
and the protection of a wall monopolized by ivy which left on its plaster
the indelible mark of its pistil

In her dreams my mother made stacks
of houses without walls
of words without syllables
of dead stars which only shone for her sleep
keeping the gardens for insomniac nights
when it was imperative to convene the nightingales
to tell them her dream which they'd pass down from father to son

My mother opened her wardrobe to dead leaves which traveled
    far from their branches
folding them into the weave of her sheets
hems and veins dressed in the same darknesses
The key made a weird sound when a ragged forest appeared at the door

to claim its share of the linens' shade
leaving its soil-mark of shame on our doorstep.

Give me a star to light my lamp
some salt to preserve the shutters' tears
some oil to soothe the doors' wounds
two arms to bury the fear-frozen bread

Your voice, mother, addressing God through the skylight
made the soil bite the pomegranate tree

My mother wandered so far in her dreams
that we found her bed empty even of
sheets which she took with her to those lands trod by her sleeping feet
where she lost her bracelets and her soul
all rediscovered under her pillow with the invisible guidebook of her sleep

My mother who would lose herself in the fire
gave our house over to the affliction of winter
and the shadow of the streetlight playing sextant

We had to look for her in the earth where she'd made her den
cry out her name along the stones
frighten our own voices and the echo which had seen my mother and the fire . . .
    pass by.

Translated by Marilyn Hacker

Joseph Brodsky

Recommended by Valzhyna Mort

This is one of my favorite poems in the Russian language. It is a love poem to a woman that turns into a declaration of love to a place—a remote, bare, dying-out village.

You've forgotten that village lost in the rows and rows
(from *A Part of Speech*)

You've forgotten that village lost in the rows and rows
of swamp in a pine-wooded territory where no scarecrows
ever stand in orchards: the crops aren't worth it,
and the roads are also just ditches and brushwood surface.
Old Nastasya is dead, I take it, and Pesterev, too, for sure,
and if not, he's sitting drunk in the cellar or
is making something out of the headboard of our bed:
a wicket gate, say, or some kind of shed.
And in winter they're chopping wood, and turnips is all they live on,
and a star blinks from all the smoke in the frosty heaven,
and no bride in chintz at the window, but dust's gray craft,
plus the emptiness where once we loved.

Translated by the author

DMITRI PRIGOV
Recommended by Vera Pavlova

True art means oneness of form and content, Hegel warns us. Dmitri Prigov with his poem "I'm tired already on the first line . . ." pleases Hegel more than any other poet. Form here describes itself and appears to be the poem's only content. Form and content cannot be more identical than they are here! This poem is truly one of a kind—a poetic version of Malevich's *Black Square*. (Variations are nevertheless possible.) For instance, here's my haiku:

> This poem
> I won't write it down
> Will leave it for myself

I'M TIRED ALREADY ON THE FIRST LINE . . .

> I'm tired already on the first line
> Of the first quatrain
> Now I've reached the third line
> And now the fourth I've reached
>
> Now I've reached the first line
> But already of the second quatrain
> Now I've reached the third line
> And now the end, O Lord, I've reached

AN EAGLE FLIES OVER THE EARTH . . .

An eagle flies over the earth
Isn't Stalin its name?
'Course not, its name is eagle
And Stalin doesn't fly up there
There's a swan flying over the earth
Isn't Prigov his name?
No, Prigov, alas, isn't its name
And Prigov isn't flying up there
What about Prigov? He sits on the earth
And steals a look up at the sky
The eagle and the swan he sees
And Stalin? He's lying in the earth

Translated by Gerald Stanton Smith

TOMAŽ ŠALAMUN

Recommended by Nikola Madzirov

It is not easy to be a fish, to live within your own silence and eye, to accept the truth older than the cross, to be God who will save many people from hunger and loneliness, and in the meantime to remember, to write, as one cannot retell and see far away, into space, into history. It is not easy to come from the womb of one's mother headfirst with a strong voice and to slide into the mouth of the world so that silence can be born. With Tomaž Šalamun, we have long discussed writing, silence, and translating silence: "I'm happiest in my sleep and when I write." You are right, Tomaž. Writing is an awake dream.

THE FISH

I am a carnivore, but a plant.
I am God and man in one.
I'm a chrysalis. Mankind grows out of me.
My brain is liquefied like
a flower, so I can love better. Sometimes I dip
my fingers in it and it's warm. Nasty people
say others have drowned
in it. Not true. I am a belly.
I put up travelers in it.
I have a wife who loves me.
Sometimes I'm afraid she loves me
more than I love her and I get sad and
depressed. My wife breathes like a small
bird. Her body soothes me.
My wife is afraid of other guests.
I say to her, now, now, don't be afraid.
All our guests are a single being, for both of us.
A white match with a blue head has fallen into my
typewriter. My nails are all dirty.
I'm thinking hard now what to write.
One of my neighbors has terribly noisy

children. I am God, I calm them down.
At one I'm going to the dentist, Dr. Mena,
Calle Reloj. I'll ring the bell and ask him
to pull my tooth, because it hurts too much.
I'm happiest in my sleep and when I write.
The masters pass me along from hand to hand.
That's essential. It's just as essential as
growing is for trees. A tree needs earth.
I need earth so I won't go mad.
I'll live four hundred and fifty years.
Tarzs Rebazar has been alive six hundred.
I don't know if that was him in the white coat,
I still can't make them out. When I write I have
a different bed. Sometimes I start pouring out more like
water, because water is most loving of all.
Fear injures people. A flower is softest
if you close your hand around it. Flowers like
hands. I like everything. Last night I
dreamed my father leaned across toward
Harriet. Other women frighten me, and
so I don't sleep with them. But the distance between
God and young people is slight.
There's always just a single woman in God, and that's
my wife. I'm not afraid of my guests tearing
me apart. I can give them anything, it will just grow back.
The more I give, the more it grows back. Then it launches off
as a source of help for other creatures. On some planet
there's a central storehouse for my flesh. I don't know
which one it's on. Whoever drinks it will
be happy. I'm a water hose. I'm God, because
I love. Everything dark in here, inside, nothing
outside. I can X-ray any creature.
I'm rumbling. When I hear the juices in my

body, I know I'm in a state of grace. I would have to
consume money day and night if I wanted to
build a life, and still it wouldn't help. I was made to
shine. Money is death. I'll go out on the terrace.
From there I can see the whole countryside as far as Dolores
Hidalgo. It's warm and soft as Tuscany,
though it's not Tuscany. Metka and I sit there,
watching. Her hands are like Shakti's. My
mouth is like some Egyptian beast's. Love is
all. Moses's wicker basket never
struck the rocks. Miniature horses come
trotting out of the level countryside. A wind blows
from the Sierras. I slide headfirst into people's
mouths and kill and give birth,
kill and give birth, because I write.

Translated by Michael Biggins

MICHAEL KRÜGER
Recommended by Nikola Madzirov

When after many years I returned to live in the room of my childhood, I had to move out of there all the pillars made of books. I had the feeling that the house would fall over me, that the architecture of the sky would remain the only non-holy palimpsest for all the locked memories. The smell of emptiness was covering the silence of cobwebs.

MIGRATION

Now the rooms are empty, the suitcases
line the corridor next to moody boxes
in which books struggle with newspapers.
An unequal battle: paper against paper,
the sequel to an old tragedy.

How strong is the smell of emptiness! A fly
makes its rounds and takes pictures,
an angel with a black flag
devoted to a droning liturgy.
On the windowsill a coin of the old
currency pays for everything.

No chair, no bed begs for mercy anymore,
even memory has vanished into thin air
like the roaches. Did someone live here?
Soon evening will move into the rooms
and erase the imprint of pictures,
pictures we took down
to never hang them up again.

Translated by Monika Zobel

Josip Osti

Recommended by Nikola Madzirov

A poem that penetrates time as if with a blade. A parallel reflexive narration that opens the gates of childhood and history through the primordial silences, sounds and images. Time is in the rust of the bayonet that can intoxicate the blood and in the shadow of the weeds that suck the nourishment from the wheat. The only sign of life is the dialogue with the wood-owl that comes from the darkness of prehistoric times, whose voice could be the cry of pain of the person into whose flesh the bullet sank about hundred years ago. The war unites all times and verbs in the lines of Josip Osti, in particular after his leaving his home in Bosnia. "After the war we're building a house . . . Day / and night, although we're only too aware that we are / building tomorrow's ruins" (Osti, "Building a House After the War").

WITH A RUSTY BAYONET FROM WORLD WAR ONE

With a rusty bayonet from World
War One I weed the garden. Thrusting
it deeply into the soil as it might have been thrust
into hard bread or soft human flesh in the times
long cleansed from its
memory. When its former shine
mirrored the fear and uncertainty
of the beautiful young man who,
at the war cemetery, has for decades
been feeding flowers and weeds
as nameless as himself . . . With a rusty bayonet
from World War One I weed the garden . . .
Pulling out nettles, dandelion . . . When the bayonet
touches a brass cartridge in the soil
I blow in it the way I learned as a child.
The silence of the Karst is broken by an unusual sound
to which a wood-owl responds. A wood-owl
whose measured, ominous voice
fills the air all night long.

Translated by Evald Flisar

ADAM ZAGAJEWSKI

Recommended by Valzhyna Mort

"To Go to Lvov" is the hymn to the city this Polish poet will never know, a hymn sung by the children of exile, born in countries that continue to exist only in their birth certificates. Forever lost, beautiful, and dreamlike, Zagajewski's Lvov is Atlantida, Jerusalem, and the Garden of Eden. His voyage for Lvov starts at the first possibility, at the birth of trains, when suitcases are still covered with dew. Whether it's a good time or not, it doesn't matter. The only thing that can stop the poet is the non-existence of his destination—his biggest fear. Lvov has to appear in front of him in all perfection of the poet's memory: from poplars and ash that breathe life into the city to invisible snails eternally discussing eternity so that the rest can enjoy their morning coffee without worrying about the metaphysical. Cut up with the scissors of history, Zagajewsky's Lvov is no longer there—that's why he has to hurry to pack and leave before he realizes he's going to nowhere.

TO GO TO LVOV

To go to Lvov. Which station
for Lvov, if not in a dream, at dawn, when dew
gleams on a suitcase, when express
trains and bullet trains are being born. To leave
in haste for Lvov, night or day, in September
or in March. But only if Lvov exists,
if it is to be found within the frontiers and not just
in my new passport, if lances of trees
—of poplar and ash—still breathe aloud
like Indians, and if streams mumble
their dark Esperanto, and grass snakes like soft signs
in the Russian language disappear
into thickets. To pack and set off, to leave
without a trace, at noon, to vanish
like fainting maidens. And burdocks, green
armies of burdocks, and below, under the canvas
of a Venetian café, the snails converse

about eternity. But the cathedral rises,
you remember, so straight, as straight
as Sunday and white napkins and a bucket
full of raspberries standing on the floor, and
my desire which wasn't born yet,
only gardens and weeds and the amber
of Queen Anne cherries, and indecent Fredro.
There was always too much of Lvov, no one could
comprehend its boroughs, hear
the murmur of each stone scorched
by the sun, at night the Orthodox church's silence was unlike
that of the cathedral, the Jesuits
baptized plants, leaf by leaf, but they grew,
grew so mindlessly, and joy hovered
everywhere, in hallways and in coffee mills
revolving by themselves, in blue
teapots, in starch, which was the first
formalist, in drops of rain and in the thorns
of roses. Frozen forsythia yellowed by the window.
The bells pealed and the air vibrated, the cornets
of nuns sailed like schooners near
the theater, there was so much of the world that
it had to do encores over and over,
the audience was in frenzy and didn't want
to leave the house. My aunts couldn't have known
yet that I'd resurrect them,
and lived so trustfully, so singly;
servants, clean and ironed, ran for
fresh cream, inside the houses
a bit of anger and great expectation, Brzozowski
came as a visiting lecturer, one of my
uncles kept writing a poem entitled *Why*,
dedicated to the Almighty, and there was too much

of Lvov, it brimmed the container,
it burst glasses, overflowed
each pond, lake, smoked through every
chimney, turned into fire, storm,
laughed with lightning, grew meek,
returned home, read the New Testament,
slept on a sofa beside the Carpathian rug,
there was too much of Lvov, and now
there isn't any, it grew relentlessly
and the scissors cut it, chilly gardeners
as always in May, without mercy,
without love, ah, wait till warm June
comes with soft ferns, boundless
fields of summer, i.e., the reality.
But scissors cut it, along the line and through
the fiber, tailors, gardeners, censors
cut the body and the wreaths, pruning shears worked
diligently, as in a child's cutout
along the dotted line of a roe deer or a swan.
Scissors, penknives, and razor blades scratched,
cut, and shortened the voluptuous dresses
of prelates, of squares and houses, and trees
fell soundlessly, as in a jungle,
and the cathedral trembled, people bade goodbye
without handkerchiefs, no tears, such a dry
mouth, I won't see you anymore, so much death
awaits you, why must every city
become Jerusalem and every man a Jew,
and now in a hurry just
pack, always, each day,
and go breathless, go to Lvov, after all
it exists, quiet and pure as
a peach. It is everywhere.

Translated by Renata Gorczyńska

PIOTR SOMMER

Recommended by Valzhyna Mort

This short poem by Polish poet Piotr Sommer is simple and straightforward. The humor and the simplicity of the poem are, however, balanced by the sensation of real terror. The power of the milkwoman over a customer who cannot find his receipt seems ridiculous and absurd. Nevertheless, she acts like a secret policeman, knocking on the door at an ungodly time of four a.m., dressed "in plain clothes" (a detail that instantly takes the reader back to Poland under martial law).

DON'T SLEEP, TAKE NOTES

At four in the morning
the milkwoman was knocking
in plain clothes, threatening
she wouldn't leave us anything,
at most remove the empties,
if I didn't produce the receipt.

It was somewhere in my jacket,
but in any case I knew
what the outcome would be:
she'd take away yesterday's curds,
she'd take the cheese and eggs,
she'd take our flat away,
she'd take away the child.

If I don't produce the receipt,
if I don't find the receipt,
the milkwoman will cut our throats.

Translated by H.J. and D.J Enright

NICHITA DANILOV
Recommended by Valzhyna Mort

Nichita Danilov is a Romanian poet who comes from a family of Russian Old Believers. He is mystic and surrealist whose religious poetry makes him stand out from the witty and ironic Romanian authors familiar to American readers. The imagination behind *Nine Variations for the Organ* to which the poems below belong reminds me of Italo Calvino and Milorad Pavić.

CYRIL

    Cyril the monk lives inside a well and writes a black psalter.
He has lived there since the age of Constantine. Around him,
the water has parted, leaving the walls wet and cold. He warms
his hands from time to time at a stone lamp. On the right
corner of his table, a blind bird pecks at a small plate of seeds.

    I lean over the side of the well, and watch him, very carefully: everything that he writes, I copy into another psalter.
Occasionally he raises his eyes toward me, but he does not
say anything.

    Sometimes the water ripples, and I cannot see what he is
writing. Then I have to lean farther over the edge.
    Other times the water thickens into clay, then cracks.
    Other times it boils like lava and spits fire.
    Then it slowly cools into stone,
and I wait. I sit on the well and wait
    for the stone to turn back into water.
    Sometimes it snows.
    Large flakes fall into the well. They do not melt, as they
normally do when they touch water. Instead they turn into
silver and copper coins and stick
    to the shaved scalp of Cyril the monk.

Cyril writes, but without feeling. I watch him very carefully: I cannot miss a word. Everything he writes, I copy into another psalter, using not
ink, but sand.

In front of me is an hourglass. I dip my quill in the stream of falling sand. I have to be exceptionally careful: any breath of wind
would erase everything I have written.

Someone else leans over me, copying what I write. If I look at him, he immediately puts his nose in his book, as if he is absorbed in reading.

He looks a little like both Cyril and me.

He often leans dangerously far over the well's edge. I yell at him to be careful not to fall down the shaft. He giggles at me like a crazy man.

He is Brother Ferapont.

FERAPONT

Above me is Brother Ferapont. His beard reaches down to his waist. He sees everything that I write. His linen shirt is tied around the middle with rope made
of linden bark. He looks very much like
Feodor Mihailovich Dostoevsky.

If I commit a small stylistic mistake, he drops a pebble on my head.

"Be careful, be careful, Brother Nichita," he says, "Be careful, that could be a costly mistake."

If I don't know exactly where to put a comma, or if I hesitate between a period and a comma, he corrects me.

"None of this matters at all," I tell him,

"In the modern Psalter, many punctuation marks are no longer used."

"Still, you should use them. You should. You never know. Who knows what the future will bring! You have to be very cautious, very careful. And another thing, you should fast more, attend more to yourself. Spend less time looking at women. If you want to become a Superior."

"None of this matters now," I respond,

"The times have changed, it's very different now. People don't fast any more. And about women . . ."

"Even so, don't forget what I'm telling you. Be very, very careful . . ."

Brother Ferapont has soft, blue eyes.
Although he is a sad man, I have never seen him cry.
He has a deep, rich voice, and he knows many psalms.
I would like to wet my quill in the sadness of his gaze. But he is so far above me. However high I raise my hand, I cannot reach his eyes.
Above Brother Ferapont is Brother Lazarus.

LAZARUS

Above Brother Ferapont is Brother Lazarus.
There is no one above Brother Lazarus. He is truly alone. He looks neither outside nor inside, but he sees everything. Above him
there is no more well.
Brother Lazarus is sadder than Christ. Every day, part of his body rots off and falls down through the well.
Brother Ferapont writes his psalter
after wetting his quill in Lazarus's wounds.
His wounds are as clear as well-water.

They do not fester. He writes nothing.
    But the blood that flows from his wounds
fills the well.
    His sad gaze reaches down to me,
his voice reaches down softly. He has never chided me.
    The well where I write is deep in one of his wounds. He opens his eyes, from time to time, to look at the Lazarus in the depths.
    The other Lazarus is as feeble as this one.

Translated by Sean Cotter

ELENA SHVARTS
Recommended by Vera Pavlova

A warlock, a priest, a conjurer of elements, a Saint Petersburg poet, Elena Shvarts trespasses the borders of consciousness and sub-consciousness, reality and delirium (and revelation). More than anybody else, she is able to create the images of suffering that surpass human stamina. A great example of this is her poem "A Portrait of the Blockade." Its title and subtitles allude to visual art. For me, this poem is a Russian poetic version of Picasso's *Guernica*.

A PORTRAIT OF THE BLOCKADE THROUGH GENRE PAINTING, STILL LIFE, AND LANDSCAPE

1 *Eyewitness Account (Genre)*

Past Andreevsky market
A man walks in the blockade.
Suddenly—an incredible vision:
The aroma of soup, a soup apparition!
Two stout babas
Pour the soup into plates,
People drink, and huddle closer,
Staring down into their reflected pupils.
Suddenly the police—
Knock plates out of hands,
Fire into the air:
People, you are eating human flesh!
Human meat!
The babas' chubby arms are bent back,
Led to the firing squad,
They walk and quietly howl,
And from their eyes wolfs' paws
Claw the air.
The passerby is too late to share in the soup.
A bird pecks it up from the ground—she is worse off.

And he leaves, stepping over the dead
Or walking around them, like puddles.

2 *Still Life*

Garbage dusks lap at the window.
A youth is hunched over impatiently,
Glancing at a casserole restlessly . . .
Inside it a cat gurgles!
You arrive, he calls it "rabbit,"
You eat, he laughs so savagely.
Soon he dies. In the air you quietly
Trace with coal a *nature* (o indeed!) *morte.*
A candle, a fragment of carpenter's glue,
A ration of bread, a handful of lentils.
Rembrandt! How one wants to live and pray.
Even if frozen, even if ossified.

3 *Mixed Landscape. Stairway, yard, church.*
(paper, coal, raven's blood)

Neither a brother nor a father anymore—
A shade they lead,
Their guns pressed against his tailbone.
A naked bulb dangles similarly,
A draft presses in from the basement.

Behind this damp blue paint—there's yellow, behind it green,
Do not scrape to the void, there's no need,
There stand plaster and vapors of hell.
Here, eat up, a potato pink color.
You have nothing more, blockade, my bone!
What have you eaten? Tell me:

Blue frost off of rocks,
Worms, a horse's snout,
A feline tail.
On barrels of human hands and tufts of hair
You have fed. On sparrows, on stars and smoke,
On trees, like a woodpecker,
On iron, like rust.
And in the yard they cut a man's throat with no knife,
Unceremoniously simply.
A voice leaks out of the steaming wound.
It sings of a mustard seed and a crumb of bread,
Of the soul of blood.
Under the weak northern lights
The sky walks on tumors.
The blockade eats up
The soul, like a wolf eats his paw in a snare,
As a fish eats a worm,
As bottomless wisdom eats words . . .
O, return all those carried far away
In the body of the flabby truck,
Jingling, like frozen firewood.

Good Friday. Empty, hungry church.
The Deacon's voice desiccated, he is barely alive,
Echoing shadows bring in the shroud—
The Priest rocks back his head:
"O, now I have seen, I have grasped—
You awoke from sick death,
And cannot recover, it's ruin for us all."
My blood becomes icy wine,
Ouroboros bites through his tail.
Teeth are scattered in the sky
In place of cruel stars.

Translated by James McGavran

ALEŠ DEBELJAK

Recommended by Tomaž Šalamun

There is only one younger Slovene poet who hit me completely, and this is Aleš Debeljak. When I returned from two years in Mexico in the winter of 1981, I read four lines, and this was a total hit for me, something which came from unknown space, something definitely outside of my range. I hadn't read Aleš. But after four lines of his poetry, I sensed that a new era was coming for Slovenian poetry. It was one sentence: "[. . .] astonished the thought after the scream moves into the speech." This sentence marked a new age. Four lines marked the territory as his territory, so with his first poems he was immediately the owner of the powerful position in everything.

THE CASTLE AVENUE WITH TREES

It will be this way and no other, he said. Who? The brunette,
now swallowing the afternoon fog and picking buttons
from my short sleeve shirt, it opens strangely, in a style
out of fashion. And I know: a hitchhiker who never enters! God

grant me charming words and smooth endings, grant me a slender
birch I can lean against and forget how life can humiliate us,
like a moon and flowers in the straps of a black weekend dress,
grant me trust in the possibility of a common uprising and cadence

of a blessing, once I could break it into a jubilant shout. Language
knows no private property. It will be this way and no other,
he said. Who? The brunette, who earlier was sipping beer foam,
he has friends down the hill, in the old Vodnik, he persuades me.

He doesn't know there's no need, really: I embrace a trunk and change
into white folds of bark, I am freshly peeled. Now write
the way I want, cut boldly, so it shows, the name for joy
that sprays. And a blowout. It is this way and every other.

Translated by Brian Henry

ISTVÁN KEMÉNY
Recommended by Aleš Šteger

Hungarian poet István Kemény is a poet of the long, balladic wave. His verses, formally strict and rhythmically hallucinatory, often delineate with a narrative note some intimate situation and play it so long that it freezes indelibly in the reader's memory.

THE BEE-KEEPER

I have been a bee-keeper for six thousand years
And for the past hundred years an electrician.
Once I retire I shall keep bees again.
Something should hum for me, oh hum for me,
Hum and hum and hum
Just for me.

Translated by George Gömöri

LUTZ SEILER
Recommended by Aleš Šteger

The German poet Lutz Seiler works with the edges of sounds. But this is not "sound poetry," although sonority is often the primary engine of the poems. This is poetry that radically confronts the past through small details. Lost layers of our identities, countries that have ceased to exist, forgotten places of terror, ruins of interpersonal relationships and forgotten cultural codes float to the surface in Seiler's seemingly random poems. In fact, the radical confrontation with the past is the main actor here, except that in the theater of the poem, this actor was assigned the role of prompter. If European poetry mostly moves along the trajectory of performative obviousness, which can often be quite bombastic, we have in front of us sublime restraint. This restraint hinges on strength, which in this poem establishes rhyme, unobtrusive images, brief allusions, and pointed meanings.

MY BIRTH YEAR, SIXTY-THREE, THAT

infinite series of children, attached
to the hallways' echo vault, creeping
with a stoop into the pocket

of another, unfamiliar coat, seven
full of wax with a weight inhaled
in corridors, eight

with a weight that had arisen
from urinals to heads, we had
gagarin, but gagarin

also had us, every morning the same scraping
of sleeves pursuing writing
over the benches & at noon
the clockwork of spoons, we had

table duty, milk duty, the pressure
of an empty lesson in our eyes jelly

in the ears until
it fell silent
gravity fell silent
that was the pain
in our caps

while urinating, in the protective wood
while speaking, we had
quotations: at least we held a light
up against the planet's shadow sides
first all together & then
each of us again
silently for himself, we had

no luck. so the houses collapse
we finally become
small again &
ride back into the villages of wood, of
straw, from which we came, cracked & thin
with an echo sharpened

on the wind: we say hello to gagarin, we
have no luck, departure, back
to our villages
& departing the villages
across the fields at night . . .

Translated by Andrew Shields

VERA PAVLOVA
Recommended by Valzhyna Mort

Vera Pavlova, one of Russia's best-known contemporary poets, is sharp. Her poems are short, laconic, and witty. Her diction is simple enough for a child, while her subject matter is often bedded in places from where children come. In the graciousness of her Eve's "passable situation" in this short untitled poem, we hear the voice of Pavlova's typical lyrical I, with her quirky wisdom, always too fast to forgive and commit little and big human mistakes.

UNTITLED

And God saw
it was good
And Adam saw
it was excellent
And Eve saw
it was passable.

Translated by Steven Seymour

GEORGI GOSPODINOV
Recommended by Aleš Šteger

Bulgarian poet Georgi Gospodinov is a master pointmaker, which often leads to roars of laughter. Noble humor in poetry is even rarer than good poems. Woven into the poems are Balkan self-irony, occasional absurdity, the apparent anonymity of stories—captured at certain key moments, which makes them universal—an indispensable, simple charm, and the gentle afflictions of life that lead to empathy.

MY MOTHER READS POETRY

2 packs thin ready-rolled pastry sheets
2 coffee cups butter melted
a kilogram of apples
1 cup biscuit crumbs
1 cup ground walnuts
2 coffee cups sugar
1 packet cinnamon powder
Wash the apples, peel
and remove the seeds, grate
in large strips, mix
with the sugar, the ground walnuts
and the cinnamon.
Take a pastry sheet,
grease it
and cover it with another sheet.
Spread some of the apple mix
over them and roll
them together. Repeat
with the other pastry sheets.
Grease them and bake
over medium heat, until

the top crust is red,
and the bottom pink.

When you bake it, it's a strudel,
but for now it's still a poem.

Translated by Maria Vassileva

MATTHIAS GÖRITZ

Recommended by Tomaž Šalamun

To become a poet is to step into the void, to jump into the dark, to make some kind of treason toward your education, toward your parents.

FROM AN OLD SUIT

My father was a suitable man
He always had things in his pockets
Chocolate for satyrs
fat polished coins for the ferryman

You certainly couldn't impress him
with a poem
with a scowling face
with nice dry socks and the promise
all would remain as it was

He knew: nothing would remain as it was
everyone would leave him
shutting him up in loneliness
lulling him into somnolent
slumber, slumber

Even the album makes a noise: it goes boom
Even the grave is a room
And even his suit, or so he imagined—
one day the worms would read it
with their tongues

Translated by Susan Bernofsky

Maxim Amelin

Recommended by Vera Pavlova

Poetry of the twenty-first century, what will it be like? This is the question posed by one of its future representatives, Maxim Amelin, a forty-year-old poet from Moscow. He is one of the most distinguished poets of his generation. As a traditionalist, he falls back on pre-Pushkinian syllabic meters, which paradoxically make his poems sound remarkably fresh and novel. Amelin is a man of exceptional erudition: he knows both Latin and ancient Greek and has authored a brilliant new translation of *The Book of Catullus of Verona*.

The poem I have selected is self-explanatory. I will limit myself to clarifying two points: the explosion in the Moscow Metro on February 6, 2004, killed forty-one persons, not counting the terrorist. "The philosopher of the common cause" in the text refers to Nikolai Fedorov (1829–1903), a seminal Russian thinker whose extravagant theories envisaged unending life, reconstitution of the dead, and their reunion with the living.

(UNTITLED)

amelin

> *how dare you*
> *write poetry*
> *after 9/11*
> —A. Vasilevskiy

Every blooming day, save Sundays and holidays
when it makes no sense to leave home to go downtown,
unless for a pressing reason, the subway with unbearable
racket, din, squealing, scraping, and clanking that grate
on eardrums and drill right through them, snatches me up

and whisks me as usual at breakneck speed past the spot
between the Avtozavodskaya and Paveletskaya stations,
the very spot where a friend of mine, not a close friend,

a quiet chap, a real family man (a rarity these days),
a great drinking companion, and a bookworm
whose honest work had not brought him
a single penny in savings, whose name was
Boris Gelibter (remember that name in your prayers,
the living), was blown to shreds by a bomb blast
on Friday, February 6, Anno Domini twenty-o-four,

at eight thirty-two in the morning, on the way
to work, during the rush hour, and the poor man
knew not that he was destined to end up, fifty-four
days prior to his forty-third birthday (o the absurd
coincidence!), in the thick of it, which at times

drives me to cursing in anger: "Those who without
a shudder gave the terrible order, and those who
knowingly and deliberately carried it out, may they
never know peace neither here nor in the hereafter,
may their bodies enjoy no sleep, neither in cold graves

nor in hot beds, may their souls be punished harshly!"—
and at times I humbly reckon that it is not our lot
to grasp the mysterious ways of heaven, that in vain
we apply to them our earthly yardsticks, that birth, life,
and death of mortals are in the hands of the Creator

who calls all the blessed back: "May those I love
abide by me!"—and at times
dark premonitions overwhelm me: if it turns out
that the philosopher of the common cause is right,
and the future resurrection will require exact and

measurable evidence, it is available here, and in refutation
of bitter claims of some thinkers it will be possible
to prove that after Auschwitz, the Gulag, after the bloodshed
of upheavals and wars, after Hiroshima, Baghdad, New York
poems indeed can be written, but of what kind?—who knows,—maybe like this one.

Translated by Steven Seymour

Tomasz Różycki
Recommended by Aleš Šteger

Polish poet Tomasz Różycki (1970) became widely known with his verse novel *Twelve Stations* (*Dwanaście Stacji*). His poetry is a meeting place of Catholicism and Silesian everyday life, formal bravura and gestures, which puts the reader in a corner. I think that one of the intentions of this poetry is to approach the universal—what connects us and what we all share. "Religions are poems," says Les Murray in "Poetry and Religion." Różycki's religion is the clear, unobtrusive privacy of grief.

Totems and Beads

It's all post-German—my post-German town
and my post-German woods, post-German graves,
post-German living room, post-German stairs
and clock face, dresser, plate, post-German car

and shirt and cup and trees and radio,
and right here on this rubbish heap I've built
my life, right here on refuse where I'll reign,
consuming and digesting this debris.

It's up to me to build a homeland from it,
but all I do is turn out oxygen
and nitrogen and carbon, live in soot-
soaked air, my element. Now look: a breeze

is lifting me. I will self-propagate,
occupy attics, pantries, suburbs, wastelands.

Scorched Maps

I took a trip to Ukraine. It was June.
I waded in the fields, all full of dust
and pollen in the air. I searched, but those
I loved had disappeared below the ground,

deeper than decades of ants. I asked
about them everywhere, but grass and leaves
have been growing, bees swarming. So I lay down,
face to the ground, and said this incantation—

you can come out, it's over. And the ground,
and moles and earthworms in it, shifted, shook,
kingdoms of ants came crawling, bees began
to fly from everywhere. I said come out,

I spoke directly to the ground and felt
the field grow vast and wild around my head.

Translated by Mira Rosenthal

LIDIJA DIMKOVSKA
Recommended by Aleš Šteger

Macedonian poet Lidija Dimkovska (1971) is relatively well-known in the U.S., but in spite of this, it seems to me that her poem should not be missing from this selection. Between Walt Disney and the metaphysics of everyday life, between the revolt of shopping centers and the spirit of investigating gender relations, the poems of Lidija Dimkovska are humorous, densely woven networks of images and cultural references, and full of making insights and vehement gestures that illuminate our everyday lives.

THE POETICS OF LIFE

I no longer speak in human languages.
I'm free as a fax message. Legible—illegible,
it will get where it should. I'll arrive in time
to plunge my knees into the caste-mark of the stove
and Krishna will start smelling of a "Quatro stagione" pizza.
How long can the bat in me keep
From appearing in front of the guests, now, when it can see in the daytime, too
(after the operation at the Fyodorov Eye Clinic in Moscow),
without having my aunt mix the radishes with the meat
fried in human fat? That's my favorite diet.
Saul told me: you won't end up in an oven, but you won't end up
in the catalogue of the National Library either.
One must earn in order to live!
Yes? So many tasks, God, there's no time even to kill oneself.
The diary is over-full with events, everything's under control,
only the controllers are nowhere to be seen: all day long they just hang about
in the supermarket where I arrange the bottles of holy water.
They buy it wholesale and resell it for metaphysical freedom.
My time is still nowhere to be seen. Summer and winter
I stand by the road and wait for it. But still it doesn't come.
It neither sends word, nor does it return.
The migrant workers, even when they were not coming back, would at least send
a pouch of money. Look at these varicose veins!

And the skin is like orange peel,
which not even the most expensive cellulite gel will smooth!
Is this how one pays for the exile called poetry?
Circles under the eyes
without the eyes, *Mademoiselle Pogany* in the arms of Walt Disney,
Paris that is not Paris when I don't think of it. I'll spend all day tomorrow
kneeling in front of the Dictionary of Religions and praying
that the wife of the priest who will marry me will die.
If I am to live to see old age,
I might at least have Paul who tangled up the threads not only
of the Corinthians, but of the extraterrestrials as well, remarry me.
Surely, my time will come too!
High state officials have said that in their statements. I took off my glasses
so as to be alone. How heartily they will laugh once they understand me!
How dear I shall become to them! Like a lottery jackpot,
like the recognition of the name of my country,
like a world of no borders shall my cross be to them.
It's just that I don't know if I believe you, babies,
that all you're doing is play,
that you won't bite off my magic finger!

Translated by Ljubica Arsovska and Peggy Reid

ANDREI KHADANOVICH
Recommended by Valzhyna Mort

Andrei Khadanovich is a one-man orchestra of Belarusian literature. He is a widely loved poet, translator, essayist, critic, and mentor, as well as a big champion of slam poetry in Eastern Europe. This poem, written during the poet's stay at the Iowa Writers' Workshop, appeals to me with its clarity and refreshing humor.

LABOR DAY

The city has stopped. Offices are closed.
Banks are closed. Money exchange is closed.
Bookstores are closed. Music stores are closed.
Drugstores are closed. I won't even ask about hospitals.

Green traffic lights are almost not working.
Mufflers on motorcycles aren't working.
Police only pretends to be working
otherwise we would have been stopped three times.

Road service is not working. Firemen are not working.
Somebody has forgotten to turn off the Southern sun
and our overheated brains are absolutely not working.

(It's enough to take a look at this poem.)

Lifeguards on Lake Michigan are not working
because the potential drowning men are not working.
Internet in our coffee shop
at the top of a Chicago skyscraper
is not even worth mentioning.

Nothing works today. America celebrates the Labor Day.

And only a spider, swayed by the wind, outside
our 96th floor window, labors on its web.

Translated by Valzhyna Mort

Milan Djordjević

Recommended by Tomaž Šalamun

Every true poet is a monster. He destroys people and their speech.

Barbarians

I'm telling you friend, barbarians are coming
to refresh the blood of mountain brooks,
with clubs to work over the weary statues and shout:
Run along into History! The barbarians
have sun in their eyes and pockets full of leek.
They mumble to themselves while they read and then
immediately make severe aesthetic judgments.
They are wet behind the ears and sentimental.
They look with suspicion on otters and lions.
Mustachioed barbarians are liberating us from cotton.
From living corpses and orchids
they'll wipe off makeup and powder.
They slap the enemies of the people, vampires,
and then with ballet dancers
make talented children, future Satanists.

Translated by Charles Simic

NIKOLA MADZIROV
Recommended by Tomaž Šalamun

When I came out of jail, people from the Secret Service—the UDBA—said, "Oh, you lost your steam, you don't write any protest poems anymore." My second book, still published by myself, was about butterflies, about nothing. It was more subversive than if I had written protest poems, since the government needed to show its pluralism and democracy. One has to be very precise not to be corrupt or used. I was fighting to be free within my writing. And just *this* was subversive, and therefore political. Yet, during the Balkan wars, when Brodsky and Miłosz were able to write something, I was completely silent. I didn't write a line of anything from 1989 to 1994. I just stopped writing. I think if you did intend to show that anger or depression, you wouldn't be able to write good poetry. But just being what you are, to be free within your writing, this is also the center of the real responsibility of the world. Therefore, your freedom is a political act.

SHADOWS PASS US BY

We'll meet one day,
like a paper boat and
a watermelon that's been cooling in the river.
The anxiety of the world will
be with us. Our palms
will eclipse the sun and we'll
approach each other holding lanterns.

One day, the wind won't
change direction.
The birch will send away leaves
into our shoes on the doorstep.
The wolves will come after
our innocence.
The butterflies will leave
their dust on our cheeks.

An old woman will tell stories
about us in the waiting room every morning.
Even what I'm saying has
been said already: we're waiting for the wind
like two flags on a border.

One day every shadow
                              will pass us by.

Translated by Magdalena Horvat

SERHIJ ZHADAN

Recommended by Valzhyna Mort

Serhij Zhadan's poems hit very close to home with me. To his "our country is not big enough for us to miss each other, / our air space is not vast enough / for us to listen to different kinds of music," I want to add that our lives as young people in Eastern Europe in the 1980s and 1990s were not different enough for me not to respond to his poetry as fast as one would respond to a familiar smell or taste. Zhadan is the singer of the post-Soviet generation, of mechanics and alcoholics, of the often "she" voyaging from bed to train to dreams with all her birthmarks, hair, and memories. His God is never a spiritual beginning, but just another mechanic, simply saner and less visible, who, with his nail, cuts the grooves on the vinyl records with Western music—His way of communication with the rest of the world.

from "STONES" (excerpts)

I

We speak of the cities we lived in—
that went into night like ships into the winter sea,

we speak of the cities that suddenly lost their ability to resist—
in front of our
eyes, like a circus show where every acrobat
dies, and so does each laughing clown; enchanted,
you watch,
never turning away (and inconspicuously
on the circus set
you grow up).

[...]

Now we remember: janitors and the night-sellers of bread,
gray, like wrapping paper,
burglerers,
taxi drivers with klaxons instead of hearts,

children who grew up
among the old furniture
(furniture smelled of poplar trees and sea).

Our city of workers and ugly middle-men,
tearjerking market beggars
who cleared
the autumn fog
with their shouts.

We got to soak in the rain
with strangers
on tram stops,
old proletarian quirks, subway cars,
we got to soak in the rain
on cars
loaded with the unemployed
like shops with catrigies.

[…]

And now we speak of those who took away our cities,
our cities
dying off like house pets,

And now we speak of those who took
our keys
(the keys we used to open the doors of the hospitals,
and walk between light
and dark of the morning pharmacies)
where every morning
the sun
was being set aflame
with all the painkillers of this earth.

[...]

Who came to power in our cities?

Who are these
clowns
that decide
to break the hearts of our houses and let out their warm raspberry blood?

Their politics
is glass chips which they scatter under their feet,
and make us
follow them.
Their politics is ropes instead of ties
on their necks,
firm ropes good for hanging them on when they exit the game.

Now they come
together in their black suits, looking like chimney-sweepers
who have come
to power.
And now they don't know where to begin.

Translated by Valzhyna Mort

An Editor's Note

The introductions to Tomaž Šalamun's recommendations were taken from the following previous personal interviews:

Henry, Brian, and Zawacki, Andrew, eds. *The Verse Book of Interviews*. Verse Books, 2005 (now Wave Books).

Simic, Charles and Šalamun, Tomaž. "Charles Simic and Tomaž Šalamun." *BOMBSITE*.

Šalamun, Tomaž. "Folk Song." Trans. Charles Simic. Ed. Henry R. Cooper. *A Bilingual Anthology of Slovene Literature*. Bloomington: Slavica Pub., 2003.

Vera Pavlova's introductions are translated from Russian by Steven Seymour.

Some of Aleš Šteger's introductions are translated from Slovenian by Brian Henry.

This book won't exist in its present form without the dedication and knowledge of people who worked alongside me and often ahead of me. My deepest gratitude is to Beth Allen, Jessica Kovler, Shaudee Lundquist, Frederick Courtright, and Ilya Kaminsky. Thank you to The Poetry Foundation for bringing together our contributing poets, Adam Zagajewski, Aleš Šteger, Eugenijus Ališanka, Nikola Madzirov, Tomaž Šalamun, and Vera Pavlova, whose work and friendship inspired this book. Thank you to all of our loved ones.

Valzhyna Mort

Contributors

Eugenijus Ališanka was born in Barnaul (Russia) in 1960. He graduated from Vilnius University, and in 1995, became a fellow of the International Writers' Workshop in Iowa. He has been Editor-in-Chief of *The Vilnius Review* and published six poetry collections, four books of essays, and translations of works by Zbigniew Herbert, Aleš Debeljak, Adam Zagajewski, Kerry Shaw Keys, and others. His poems have been translated into more than twenty languages. And in the United States, he has published *City of Ash* (Northwestern University Press 2000) and *From Unwritten Histories* (Host Publications 2011).

Nikola Madzirov was born in 1973 in Strumica, Macedonia. His award-winning poetry has been translated into thirty languages and published in the United States, Europe, and Asia. In 2011, BOA Editions published a selection of his poetry entitled *Remnants of Another Age*. In the foreword, Carolyn Forché writes, "Madzirov calls himself 'an involuntary descendant of refugees,' referring to his family's flight from the Balkan Wars a century ago: his surname derives from mazir or majir, meaning 'people without a home.' The ideas of shelter and of homelessness, of nomadism, and spiritual transience serve as a palimpsest in these Remnants."

Valzhyna Mort was born in Minsk, Belarus, and moved to the United States in 2006. She is the author of two collections of poetry, *Factory of Tears* (Copper Canyon Press 2008) and *Collected Body* (Copper Canyon Press 2011). She is the recipient of the Lannan Foundation Fellowship and the Bess Hokin Prize from *Poetry Magazine*.

Vera Pavlova was born in Moscow. She graduated from the Gnessin Academy, specializing in the history of music, and is the author of fourteen collections of poetry, four opera librettos, and lyrics to two cantatas. In the United States, Pavlova's poems have appeared in *Verse*, *Tin House*, *The New Yorker*, and *Poetry* Magazine, as well as *The New York Times*. Her first collection in English, *If There Is Something to Desire*, was published to a wide acclaim by Alfred A. Knopf in 2010.

Tomaž Šalamun lives in Ljubljana, Slovenia. He taught Spring Semester 2011 at the Michener Center for Writers at The University of Texas. His recent books translated into English are *Woods and Chalices* (Harcourt 2008), *Poker* (Ugly

Duckling Presse second edition, 2008), *There's the Hand and There's the Arid Chair* (Counterpath Press 2009), *The Blue Tower* (Houghton Mifflin Harcourt 2011), and most recently, *On the Tracks of Wild Game* (Ugly Duckling Presse, 2012).

ALEŠ ŠTEGER is a Slovenian writer and translator. He has published five books of poetry (most recently *Knjiga teles*, 2010) as well as essays and fiction, and is a translator from German and Spanish. He currently works in Ljubljana as Editor-in-Chief of the Beletrina Academic Press and as one of the program directors for Maribor 2012 European Capital of Culture. Visit him online at www.alessteger.com.

ADAM ZAGAJEWSKI, born in Lvov (Ukraine), lived for twenty years in Paris and in 2002 returned to Krakow. In the spring of 1988, he began teaching at the University of Houston. In 2007, he became a member of the Committee on Social Thought at the University of Chicago, where he currently teaches one quarter per year. He has published several volumes of poems, and his essays have been translated into many languages. His most recent publication is a new collection of poetry, *Unseen Hand*.

Permissions

Abdullaev, Shamshad. "Summer, Landscape." Translated by Valzhyna Mort. Reprinted by permission of Valzhyna Mort and Shamshad Abdullaev.

Amelin, Maxim. "Untitled." Translated by Steven Seymour. Reprinted by permission of Steven Seymour and Maxim Amelin.

Anonymous. "Euphrosyne's Incantation." In *The Song of Igor's Campaign*. Translated by Vladimir Nabokov. Copyright © 1960 by Vladimir Nabokov. The Overlook Press. Published 2003 by Ardis Publishers. Reprinted by permission of Ardis Publishers/The Overlook Press. All rights reserved.

Apollinaire, Guillaume. "The Pretty Redhead." In *Collected Poems of James Wright*. Translated by James Wright. Copyright © 1971 by James Wright. Reprinted by permission of Wesleyan University Press, www.wesleyan.edu/wespress.

Aygi, Gennady. "People." In *Into the Snow: Selected Poems of Gennady Aygi*. Translated by Sarah Valentine. Copyright © 2011 by the Estate of Gennady Aygi. Translation copyright © 2011 by Sarah Valentine. Reprinted by permission of Wave Books and the translator.

Benn, Gottfried. "Chopin." In *Twentieth Century German Poetry*. Edited and translated by Michael Hofmann. Copyright © 2005 by Michael Hofmann. Reprinted by permission of Farrar, Straus, and Giroux, LLC.

Białoszewski, Miron. "And Even, Even If They Take Away the Stove." In *Post-War Polish Poetry*. Translated by Czesław Miłosz. Copyright © 1965 by Czesław Miłosz. Used by permission of The Wylie Agency, LLC.

Błożė, Vytautas P. "III." In *Preludes: Four Poets of Lithuania*. Selected and translated by Jonas Zdanys (Vilmus: Vaga 1995). Reprinted by permission of Jonas Zdanys and Vytautas Błožė.

Bonnefoy, Yves. "Place of the Salamander." In *Early Poems 1947–1959*. Translated by Galway Kinnell and Richard Pevear. Copyright © 1978 by Mercure de France. Translation copyright © 1991 by Ohio University Press. Used by permission of Ohio University Press, www.ohioswallow.com.

Brecht, Bertolt. "Of Poor B.B." Originally appeared in *Poetry* (2006). Translated by Michael Hofmann. Reprinted by permission of Michael Hofmann.

Brodsky, Joseph. "You've forgotten that village lost in the rows and rows." From "A Part of Speech" in *A Part of Speech*. Translated by Joseph Brodsky. Translation copyright © 1980 by Farrar, Straus, and Giroux, LLC. Reprinted by permission of Farrar, Straus and Giroux, LLC.

Cassian, Nina. "Temptation" and "Fairytale" In *Life Sentence: Selected Poems*. Translated by Brenda Walker and Andrea Deletant and edited by William Jay Smith. Copyright © 1990 by Nina Cassian. Used by permission of W.W. Norton & Company, Inc. "Us Two." In *Continuum: Poems*. Translated by Brenda Walker and Andrea Deletant. Copyright © 2008 by Nina Cassian. Used by permission of W.W. Norton & Company, Inc.

Catallus. "Poem 72." In *The Poems of Catallus*. Translated with an introduction by Peter Whigham. Copyright © 1966 by Penguin Books, Ltd. Reprinted by permission of Penguin Books Ltd.

Celan, Paul. "Deathfugue." In *Selected Poems and Prose of Paul Celan*. Translated by John Felstiner. Copyright © 2001 by John Felstiner. Used by permission of S. Fischer Verlag GmbH and W. W. Norton & Company, Inc.

Danilov, Nichita. "Cyril," "Ferapont," and "Lazarus." In *Second-Hand Souls: Selected Writings*. Translated by Sean Cotter. Copyright © 1993, 1999, 2000, 2003 by Nichita Danilov. Translation copyright © 2003 by Sean Cotter. Reprinted by permission of Twisted Spoon Press.

Debeljak, Aleš. "The Castle Avenue with Trees." In *Guernica*. Translated by Brian Henry. Reprinted by permission of Brian Henry and Aleš Debeljak.

Dimkovska, Lidija. "The Poetics of Life." In *Do Not Awaken Them with Hammers*. Translated by Ljubica Arsovska and Peggy Reid. Copyright © 2006 by Lidija Dimkovska. Translation copyright © 2006 by Ljubica Arsovska and Peggy Reid. Reprinted by permission of Ugly Duckling Presse.

Djordjević, Milan. "Barbarians." In *Oranges and Snow: Selected Poems of Milan Djordjević*. Translated by Charles Simic. Copyright © 2010 by Princeton University Press. Reprinted by permission of Princeton University Press.

Enzensberger, Hans Magnus. "Further Reasons Why Poets Don't Tell the Truth." In *Selected Poems*. Translated by Michael Hamburger. Reprinted by permission of Sheep Meadow Press.

Göritz, Matthias. "From an Old Suit." In *Shampoo Magazine*, No. 35 (2009). Translated by Susan Bernofsky. Copyright © 2006 Berlin Verlang GmbH. Reprinted by permission of Susan Bernofsky and Piper Verlag GmbH.

Gospodinov, Georgi. "My Mother Reads Poetry." In *Modern Poetry in Translation*, Series 3, No. 11 (2009). Translated by Maria Vassileva. Copyright © 2009 by Georgi Gospodinov. Reprinted by permission of Maria Vassileva.

Herbert, Zbigniew. "The Seventh Angel." In *Collected Poems: 1956–1998*. Translated by Czesław Miłosz and Peter Dale Scott. Copyright © 2007 by The Estate of Zbigniew Herbert. Reprinted by permission of HarperCollins Publishers.

Krüger, Michael. "Migration." Translated by Monika Zobel. Reprinted by permission of Monika Zobel and Michael Krüger.

Machado, Antonio. "Portrait." In *Border of a Dream: Selected Poems*. Translated by Willis Barnstone. Copyright © 2004 by the Heirs of Antonio Machado. English translation copyright © 2004 by Willis Barnstone. Reprinted with the permission of The Permissions Company, Inc., on behalf of Copper Canyon Press, www.coppercanyonpress.org.

Madzirov, Nikola. "Shadows Pass Us By." In *Remnants of Another Age*. Translated from the Macedonian by Peggy and Graham W. Reid, Magdalena Horvat and Adam Reed. Copyright © 2011 by Nikola Madzirov. Translation copyright © 2011 by Peggy and Graham W. Reid, Magdalena Horvat, and Adam Reed. Reprinted by permission of The Permissions Company, Inc. on behalf of BOA Editions Ltd., www.boaeditions.org.

Mandelstam, Osip. "I Was Washing in the Yard at Night." In *Circumference: Poetry in Translation 4*. Translated by Ilya Bernstein. Reprinted by permission of Ilya Bernstein.

Mihalić, Slavko. "War." In *Black Apples, Selected Poems: 1954–1987*. Translated by Bernard Johnson. Copyright © 1989 by Exile Editions. Reprinted by permission of Exile Editions.

Miłosz, Czesław. "Elegy for N.N." In *Selected Poems: 1931–2004*. Translated by Czesław Miłosz and Lawrence Davis. Copyright © 1988, 1991, 1995, 2001, 2004, 2006 by The Czesław Miłosz Estate. Reprinted by permission of HarperCollins Publishers.

Montale, Eugenio. "Letter to Malvolio." In *The Collected Poems of Eugenio Montale 1925–1977*. Edited by Rosanna Warren. Translated by William Arrowsmith. Copyright © 1973 by Arnoldo Mondadori Editore S.p.A., Milano. Translation copyright © 2012 by Beth Arrowsmith, Nancy Arrowsmith, and Rosanna Warren. Used by permission of W. W. Norton & Company, Inc and Arnoldo Mondadori Editore S.p.A., Milano.

Norwid, Cyprian. "Marionettes." Translated by Steven Seymour. Reprinted by permission of Steven Seymour.

Osti, Josip. "With a Rusty Bayonet from World War One." In *The Drunken Boat* Vol. 6, Issues III–IV (2006). Translated by Evald Flisar. Reprinted by permission of Evald Flisar and Josip Osti.

Parun, Vesna. "My Grandfather." In *Women on War: An International Anthology of Women's Writings from Antiquity to the Present*. Translated by Ivana Spalatin and Daniela Gioseffi. Reprinted by permission of Daniela Gioseffi.

Pavlova, Vera. "Untitled." In *If There is Something to Desire: One Hundred Poems*. Translated by Steven Seymour. Copyright © 2010 by Vera Pavlova. Translation copyright © 2010 by Steven Seymour. Used by permission of Alfred A. Knopf, a division of Random House, Inc. Any third party use of this material, outside of this publication, is prohibited. Interested parties must apply directly to Random House, Inc. for permission.

Pavese, Cesare. "Grappa in September." In *Disaffections: Complete Poems 1930–1950*. Translated by Geoffrey Brock. Copyright © 1998 by Giulio Einaudi editore s.p.a., Torino. Translation copyright © 2002 by Geoffrey Brock. Reprinted with the permission of The Permissions Company, Inc., on behalf of Copper Canyon Press, www.coppercanyonpress.org.

Perse, Saint-John. "V." In *Collected Poems*. Translated by T.S. Eliot. Copyright © 1971 and renewed 1999 by Princeton University Press. Reprinted by permission of Princeton University Press.

Pilinszky, János. "The French Prisoner." In *Poetry* (March 2008). Translated by Clive Wilmer and George Gömöri. Reprinted by permission of Clive Wilmer and Worple Press.

Popa, Vasko. "In the Village of My Ancestors." In *Homage to the Lame Wolf: Selected Poems*. Translated by Charles Simic. Copyright © 1987 by Oberlin College. Reprinted with the permission of Oberlin College Press.

Prigov, Dmitri. "I'm Tired Already on the First Line" and "An Eagle Flies over the Earth." In *Contemporary Russian Poetry: A Bilingual Anthology*. Translated and edited by Gerald Stanton Smith. Copyright © 1993 by Gerald Stanton Smith. Reprinted by permission of Indiana University Press.

Queneau, Raymond. "Poor Fellow" and "Toward a Poetic Art: 9." In *Pounding the Pavement, Beating the Bushes, and Other Pataphysical Poems*. Translated by Teo Savory. Reprinted by permission of Unicorn Press and Éditions Gallimard, Paris.

Rilke, Rainer Maria. "Orpheus. Eurydice. Hermes." In *The Selected Poetry of Rainer Maria Rilke*. Translated by Stephen Mitchell. Translation copyright © 1982 by Stephen Mitchell. Used by permission of Random House, an imprint and division of Random House LLC. All rights reserved.

Ritsos, Yannis. "Immobility of the Voyage." Originally appeared in *Poetry* (1964). Translated by Rae Dalven. Reprinted with permission of The Estate of Rae Dalven.

Różycki, Tomasz. "Scorched Maps." In *PEN America: A Journal for Writers and Readers*. Translated by Mira Rosenthal. Copyright © 2009 by PEN America. Reprinted by permission of PEN America. "Totems and Beads." In *Colonies*. Translated by Mira Rosenthal. Copyright © 2013 by Tomasz Różycki. English translation copyright © 2013 by Miral Rosenthal. Reprinted with the permission of The Permissions Company, Inc., on behalf of Zephyr Press, www.zephyrpress.org.

Šalamun, Tomaž. "The Fish." In *The Four Questions of Melancholy*. Translated by Michael Biggins. Copyright © 1997 by Tomaž Šalamun. Translation copyright © 1997 by Michael Biggins. Reprinted with the permission of White Pine Press, www.whitepine.org.

Sappho. ["He seems to me equal to gods that man."] In *If Not, Winter* by Anne Carson. Copyright © 2002 by Anne Carson. Used by permission of Alfred A. Knopf, a division of Random House, Inc. Any third party use of this material, outside of this publication, is prohibited. Interested parties must apply directly to Random House, Inc. for permission.

Seferis, George. "The King of Asine." In *Collected Poems*. Translated, edited, and introduced by Edmund Keeley and Philip Sherrard. Copyright © 1967 and renewed 1995 by Princeton University Press. Reprinted by permission of Princeton University Press.

Seiler, Lutz. "My Birth Year, Sixty-Three, That." Translated by Andrew Shields. Reprinted by permission of Andrew Shields and Lutz Seiler.

Shvarts, Elena. "A Portrait of a Blockade through Genre Painting, Still Life, and Landscape." In *An Anthology of Contemporary Russian Women Poets*. Translated by James McGavran and edited by Valentina Polukhina and Daniel Weissbort. Copyright © 2005 by University of Iowa Press. Reprinted by permission of University of Iowa Press.

Sommer, Piotr. "Don't Sleep, Take Notes." In *Continued*. Translated by H.J and D.J. Enright. Copyright © 2005 by Piotr Sommer. Reprinted by permission of Wesleyan University Press, www.wesleyan.edu/wespress.

Stănescu, Nichita. "Airplane Dance" and "The Fifth Elegy." In *Wheel with a Single Spoke and Other Poems*. Translated by Sean Cotter. Copyright © 2012 by Nichita Stănescu. Translation copyright © 2012 by Sean Cotter. Reprinted by permission of Archipelago Books.

Swir, Anna. "Soup for the Poor," "I Wash the Shirt," and "A Film About My Father." In *Talking to My Body*. Translated by Czesław Miłosz and Leonard Nathan. English translation copyright © 1996 by Czesław Miłosz and Leonard Nathan. Reprinted with the permission of The Permissions Company, Inc., on behalf of Copper Canyon Press, www.coppercanyonpress.org.

Szymborska, Wisława. "Cat in an Empty Apartment." In *Poems: New and Collected 1957–1997*. Translated from the Polish by Stanisław Barańczak and Clare Cavanagh. English translation copyright © 1998 by Houghton Mifflin Harcourt Publishing Company. Reprinted by permission of Houghton Mifflin Harcourt Publishing Company. All rights reserved.

Trakl, Georg. "The Sun" and "Descent and Defeat." In *The Winged Energy of Delight: Selected Translations*. Translated by Robert Bly. Copyright © 2004 by Robert Bly. Reprinted by permission of HarperCollins Publishers.

Something Indecent is part of a collaboration with the *Poets in the World* series created by The Poetry Foundation's Harriet Monroe Poetry Institute. The *Poets in the World* series supports research and publication of poetry and poetics from around the world and highlights the importance of creating a space for poetry in local communities.

THE HARRIET MONROE POETRY INSTITUTE is an independent forum created by The Poetry Foundation to provide a space in which fresh thinking about poetry, in both its intellectual and practical needs, can flourish free of allegiances other than to the best ideas. The Institute convenes leading poets, scholars, publishers, educators, and other thinkers from inside and outside the poetry world to address issues of importance to the art form of poetry and to identify and champion solutions for the benefit of the art. For more information, please visit www.poetryfoundation.org/institute.

THE POETRY FOUNDATION, publisher of *Poetry* magazine, is an independent literary organization committed to a vigorous presence for poetry in our culture. It exists to discover and celebrate the best poetry and to place it before the largest possible audience. The Poetry Foundation seeks to be a leader in shaping a receptive climate for poetry by developing new audiences, creating new avenues for delivery, and encouraging new kinds of poetry through innovative partnerships, prizes, and programs. For more information, please visit www.poetryfoundation.org.

HARRIET MONROE POETRY INSTITUTE
POETS IN THE WORLD SERIES

PUBLICATIONS

***Ilya Kaminsky**, 2011 – 2013 HMPI director*
Poets in the World *series editor*

Dawes, Kwame and Abani, Chris, eds. *Seven New Generation African Poets.* Slapering Hol Press.

Barnett, Catherine and Yanique, Tiphanie, eds. *Another English: Anglophone Poems from Around the World.* Tupelo Press.

Di, Ming, ed. *New Cathay: Contemporary Chinese Poetry.* Tupelo Press.

Griswold, Eliza, ed. "Landays: Poetry of Afghan Women." *Poetry* magazine, June 2013.

Hawkley, Jared, Rich, Susan, and Turner, Brian, eds. *The Strangest of Theatres: Poets Writing Across Borders.* McSweeney's.

Mikhail, Dunya, ed. *Fifteen Iraqi Poets.* New Directions Publishing.

Mörling, Malena and Ellerström, Jonas, eds and trans. *The Star By My Head: Poets from Sweden.* Milkweed Editions.

Mort, Valzhyna, ed. *Something Indecent: Poems Recommended by Eastern European Poets.* Red Hen Press.

Lasky, Dorothea, Luxford, Dominic, and Nathan, Jesse, eds. *Open the Door: How to Excite Young People about Poetry.* McSweeney's.

Weinberger, Eliot, ed. *Elsewhere.* Open Letter Books.

Zurita, Raúl and Gander, Forrest, eds. *Pinholes in the Night: Essential Poems from Latin America*. Copper Canyon Press.

Katharine Coles, *HMPI inaugural director*

Coles, Katharine, ed. *Blueprints: Bringing Poetry into Communities*. University of Utah Press.

Code of Best Practices in Fair Use for Poetry. Created by the Harriet Monroe Poetry Institute with American University's Center for Social Media and Washington College of Law.

Poetry and New Media: A Users' Guide. Report of the Poetry and New Media Working Group. Harriet Monroe Poetry Institute.